PRAISE FOR *HAVANAS in CAMELOT*

"An exhilarating parade of pithy, wry, and revealing true tales that remind us with a jolt of just how spirited, incisive, and spit-shined a writer Styron was. . . . Beneath the wonderfully diverting dazzle of his wit and virtuosity, Styron addresses the crucial matters of freedom, art, and empathy."

—*Booklist*

"[Styron's] love of books, [his] veneration of the printed word as a source of wisdom, redemption and refuge animates many of [the] essays in this volume, conjuring that era in which the author came of age. . . . Evocative."

—*The New York Times*

"The reader gets a rare and disarmingly personal glimpse of Styron's family relationships and friendships . . . all told in Styron's clear, distinctive voice. His easy prose, highly personal reflections, and assuming wit make this collection eminently readable, whether by a fan or a Styron novice."

—*Library Journal*

"Stylish . . . Should delight fans of Styron's best novel, *Sophie's Choice* . . . or his elegant and revealing memoir of depression, *Darkness Visible*."

—*USA Today*

ALSO BY

WILLIAM STYRON

A Tidewater Morning: Three Tales from Youth, 1993

Darkness Visible: A Memoir of Madness, 1990

This Quiet Dust, and Other Writings, 1982; expanded 1993

Sophie's Choice, 1979

The Confessions of Nat Turner, 1967

Set This House on Fire, 1960

The Long March, 1953 (serial), 1956 (book)

Lie Down in Darkness, 1951

HAVANAS in CAMELOT

HAVANAS

in CAMELOT

PERSONAL ESSAYS

WILLIAM
STYRON

RANDOM HOUSE TRADE PAPERBACKS
NEW YORK

The manuscripts of "A Literary Forefather," "Too Late for Conversion or Prayer," "Moviegoer," and "Walking with Aquinnah" are among the William Styron Papers at Duke University. The publisher is grateful to Robert L. Byrd, director of the Rare Book, Manuscript, and Special Collections Library at Duke, and to his staff for access to these papers and for other assistance in the preparation of this volume.

Published in the United States by Random House Trade Paperbacks,
an imprint of The Random House Publishing Group,
a division of Random House, Inc., New York.

RANDOM HOUSE TRADE PAPERBACKS and colophon
are trademarks of Random House, Inc.

Originally published in hardcover in the United States by Random House,
an imprint of The Random House Publishing Group,
a division of Random House, Inc., in 2008.

Most of the essays in this work are previously published. They
have appeared, some in different form, in *The Boston Globe, Egoïste,
Le Figaro, The New Yorker, The New York Times, The New York
Times Book Review, The New York Times Magazine,
The Paris Review, Traces,* and *Vanity Fair.*

Facsimile of internal memo from David L. Chambers to
Hiram Haydn used by permission from the Lilly Library, Indiana University.

LIBRARY OF CONGRESS CATALOGING-IN-PUBLICATION DATA

Styron, William, 1925–2006
Havanas in Camelot : personal essays / William Styron.
p.   cm.
ISBN 978-0-8129-7875-9
1. Styron, William, 1925–2006.   I. Title.
PS3569.T9Z468   2008
813'.54—dc22   2007028258
[B]

Printed in the United States of America

www.atrandom.com

2 4 6 8 9 7 5 3 1

Title-page photograph: © Jill Krementz, all rights reserved

Book design by Barbara M. Bachman

SEVERAL MONTHS BEFORE THE ONSET OF HIS FINAL illness, William Styron began to assemble materials for a collection of his personal essays. Most of the items in the present volume, including the title essay, are his selections. The final arrangement of the materials was made by Rose Styron, the author's widow. James L. W. West III, the author's biographer, prepared the texts for publication. "Moviegoer" and "Too Late for Conversion or Prayer" appeared initially in French translations in *Le Figaro* and *Egoïste*. They are published here for the first time in English, in texts taken from Styron's manuscripts. A portion of "A Literary Forefather" appeared in the double fiction issue of the *New Yorker* for 26 June–3 July 1995; the complete text survives among Styron's papers and is published here in full. "Walking with Aquinnah," previously unpublished, was discovered among Styron's manuscripts after his death.

CONTENTS

HAVANAS in CAMELOT

John F. Kennedy with cigar.

CECIL STOUGHTON, JOHN F. KENNEDY PRESIDENTIAL LIBRARY, BOSTON.

HAVANAS
in CAMELOT

LIKE MILLIONS OF OTHERS, I WATCHED TRANS-
fixed in late April 1996 as the acquisitive delirium that swept
through Sotheby's turned the humblest knickknack of
Camelot into a fetish for which people would pony up a fortune. A bundle of old magazines, including *Modern Screen*
and *Ladies' Home Journal*, went for $12,650. A photograph
of an Aaron Shikler portrait of Jackie—not the portrait itself, mind you, a *photo*—was sold for $41,400. (Sotheby's
had valued the picture at $50 to $75.) A Swiss "Golf-
Sport" stroke counter, worth $50 to $100 by Sotheby's estimate, fetched an insane $28,750. But surely among the
most grandiose trophies, in terms of its bloated price, was
John Kennedy's walnut cigar humidor, which Milton Berle
had given the president in 1961 after having attached a
plaque reading "To J.F.K. Good Health—Good Smoking,
Milton Berle 1/20/61." The comedian had paid $600 to
$800 for it in that year. Thirty-five years later, poor Berle

tried to buy the humidor back at Sotheby's but dropped out of the bidding at $185,000.

The winner was Marvin Shanken, publisher of the magazine *Cigar Aficionado*, who spent $574,500 on an object the auctioneers had appraised at $2,000 to $2,500. Even at such a flabbergasting price the humidor should prove to play an important mascot role in the fortunes of Shanken's magazine, which is already wildly successful, featuring (aside from cigars and cigar-puffing celebrities) articles on polo and golf, swank hotels, antique cars, and many other requirements for a truly tony lifestyle in the 1990s. After all, John F. Kennedy was no stranger to the nobby life, and what could be more appropriate as a relic for a cigar magazine than the vault in which reposed the Havanas of our last genuine cigar-smoking president?

I never laid eyes on the fabled humidor, but on the occasions I encountered Kennedy I sensed he must have owned one, protecting his precious supply, for he approached cigars with the relish and delight of—well, an aficionado. Indeed, if I allow my memory to be given a Proustian prod, and recollect Kennedy at the loose and relaxed moments when our lives briefly intersected, I can almost smell the smoke of the Havanas for which he'd developed such an impetuous, Kennedyesque weakness.

After the clunky Eisenhower years it was wonderful to have this dashing young guy in the spotlight, and soon there was nothing unusual in seeing the president posed, without apology or self-consciousness, holding a cigar. I had become friendly with two members of the Kennedy staff, Arthur Schlesinger, Jr., and Richard Goodwin, both of whom were so passionate about cigars that smoking appeared to me to be almost a White House subculture. They would lecture me about cigars whenever I saw them in Washington. Havanas were, of course, the sine qua non, and, as an ignorant cigarette smoker still clinging miserably to an unwanted addiction, I found myself fascinated but a little puzzled by all the cigar talk, by the effusive praise for a Montecristo of a certain length and vintage, by the descriptions of wrappers and their shades, by the subtle distinctions made between the flavors of a Ramon Allones and a Punch. Stubbornly, I kept up my odious allegiance to cigarettes, but in my secret heart I envied these men for their devotion to another incarnation of tobacco, one that had been transubstantiated from mere weed into an object plainly capable of evoking rapture.

IN LATE APRIL OF 1962 I was one of a small group of writers invited to what turned out to be possibly the most memorable social event of the Kennedy presidency. This was a state dinner in honor of Nobel Prize winners. Schlesinger and Goodwin were responsible for my being included—at the time, Kennedy didn't know me, as they say, from Adam—and it was a giddy pleasure for my wife, Rose, and me to head off to the White House on a balmy spring evening in the company of my friend James Baldwin, who was on the verge of becoming the most celebrated black writer in America. I recall that it was the only time I ever shaved twice on the same day.

Before dinner the booze flowed abundantly and the atmosphere crackled with excitement as J.F.K. and his beautiful lady joined the assembly and presided over the receiving line. Jack and Jackie actually *shimmered*. You would have had to be abnormal, perhaps psychotic, to be immune to their dumbfounding appeal. Even Republicans were gaga. They were truly the golden couple, and I am not trying to play down my own sense of wonder when I note that a number of the guests, male and female, appeared so affected by the glamour that their eyes took on a goofy, catatonic glaze.

Although I remained in control of myself, I got prematurely plastered; this did not damage my critical faculties when it came to judging the dinner. I'd spent a considerable amount of time in Paris and had become something of a food and wine snob. Later, in my notebook, I ungratefully recorded that while the Puligny-Montrachet 1959, served with the first course, was "more than adequate," I found the Mouton-Rothschild 1955, accompanying the *filet de boeuf* Wellington, "lacking in maturity." The dessert, something called a *bombe Caribienne*, I deemed "much too sweet, a real bomb."

Reviewing these notes so many years later, I cringe at my churlishness (including the condescending remark that the meal was "doubtless better than anything Ike and Mamie served up"), especially in view of the thrilling verve and happy spirits of the entire evening. Because of the placement of the tables I was seated at right angles to the president, and I was only several feet away when he rose from his own table and uttered his famous bon mot about the occasion representing the greatest gathering of minds at the White House since "Thomas Jefferson dined here alone." The Nobelists roared their appreciation at this elegant bouquet, and I sensed the words passing into immortality.

The White House was anything but smoke-free, and the scullions among us lit up our cigarettes. I noticed with my usual sulkiness and envy that many gentlemen at the tables around the room had begun to smoke cigars; among them was Kennedy, who was engaged in conversation with a stunning golden-haired young woman and plainly relishing her at least as much as his Churchill. Following coffee, we moved into the East Room for a concert of chamber music. After this, just as the party was breaking up and we were about to be converted into pumpkins, I was aston-

ike millions of others, I watched transfixed as the acquisitive delirium that swept through Sotheby's turned the humblest knickknack of Camelot into a fetish for which people would pony up a fortune. A bundle of old magazines, including *Modern Screen* and *Ladies' Home Journal*, went for $12,650. A photograph of an Aaron Shikler portrait of Jackie—not the portrait itself, mind you, a *photo*—was sold for $41,400. (Sotheby's had valued the picture at $50-75.) A Swiss "Golf-Sport" stroke counter, worth $50-100 by Sotheby's estimate, fetched an insane $28,750. But surely among the most grandiose trophies, in terms of its bloated price, was John Kennedy's walnut cigar humidor, which Milton Berle had given the president in 1961 after having attached a plaque reading "To J.F.K. Good Health—Good Smoking, Milton Berle 1/20/61." The comedian had paid $800 to $1,000" for it in that year. Thirty-five years later, poor Berle tried to buy the humidor back at Sotheby's but dropped out of the bidding at $185,000. The winner was Marvin Shanken, publisher of the magazine *Cigar Aficionado*, who spent $574,500 on an object the auctioneers had appraised at $2,000-2,500. Even at such a flabbergasting price the humidor should prove to play an important mascot role in the fortunes of Shanken's magazine, which is already wildly successful and sumptuously produced, featuring (aside from cigars and cigar-puffing celebrities) articles on polo and golf, swank hotels, antique cars, caviar, single-malt whiskeys, watches, straight-edge razors, tooled leather book-bindings, cologne, crystal, lighters, and many other requirements for a truly tony lifestyle in the 1990s. After all, John F. Kennedy was no stranger to the nobby life, and what could be more appropriate than as a relic for a cigar magazine than the vault in which reposed the Havanas of our last cigar-smoking president?

I never laid eyes on the fabled humidor, but on the occasions I encountered Kennedy I sensed he must have owned one, protecting his precious supply, for he approached cigars with the relish and delight of—well, an aficionado. Indeed, if I allow my memory to be given a Proustian prod, and recollect Kennedy at the loose and relaxed moments when our lives briefly intersected, I can almost smell the smoke of the Havanas

for which he'd developed such an impetuous, Kennedyesque weakness.

After the clunky Eisenhower years, it was wonderful to have this dashing young guy in the spotlight, and soon there was nothing unusual in seeing the president posed, without apology or self-consciousness, holding a cigar. I had become friendly with two members of the Kennedy staff, Arthur Schlesinger Jr. and Richard Goodwin, both of whom were so passionate about cigars that smoking appeared to me to be almost a White House subculture. They would lecture me about cigars whenever I saw them in Washington. Havanas were, of course, the sine qua non, and, as an ignorant cigarette smoker still clinging miserably to an unwanted addiction, I found myself fascinated but a little puzzled by all the cigar talk, by the effusive praise for a Montecristo of a certain length and vintage, by the descriptions of wrappers and their shades, by the subtle distinctions made between the flavors of a Ramon Allones and a Punch. Stubbornly, I kept up my odious allegiance to cigarettes, but in my secret heart I envied these men for their devotion to another incarnation of tobacco, one that had been transubstantiated from mere weed into an object plainly capable of evoking rapture.

In late April of 1962 I and a small group of literary people invited to what turned out to be possibly the most memorable social event of the Kennedy presidency. This was a state dinner in honor of Nobel Prize winners. Schlesinger and Goodwin were responsible for my being included—at the time, Kennedy didn't know me, as they say, from Adam—and it was a giddy pleasure for my wife, Rose, and me to head off to the White House on a balmy spring evening in the company of my friend James Baldwin, who was on the verge of becoming the most celebrated black writer in America. I recall that it was the only time I ever shaved twice on the same day.

Before dinner the booze flowed abundantly and the atmosphere crackled with excitement as J.F.K. and his beautiful lady joined the assembly and presided over the receiving line. Jack and Jackie actually *shimmered*. You would have had to be abnormal, perhaps psychotic, to be immune to their dumbfounding appeal. Even Republicans were gaga. They were truly the golden couple, and I am not trying to play down my own sense of wonder when I note that a number of the guests,

male and female, appeared so affected by the glamour that their eyes took on a bizarre catatonic glaze.

Although I remained in control of myself, I got prematurely plastered; this did not damage my critical faculties when it came to judging the dinner. I'd spent a considerable amount of time in Paris and had become something of a food and wine snob. Later, in my notebook, I ungratefully recorded that while the Puligny Montrachet 1959, served with the first course, was "more than adequate," I found the Mouton Rothschild 1955, accompanying the filet de boeuf Wellington, "lacking in maturity." The dessert, something called a "bombe Caribienne," I deemed "much too sweet, a real bomb."

Reviewing these notes so many years later, I cringe at my churlishness (including the condescending remark that the meal was "doubtless better than anything Ike and Mamie served up"), especially in view of the thrilling verve and happy spirits of the entire evening. Because of the placement of the tables I was seated at right angles to the president, and I was only several feet away when he rose from his own table and uttered his famous bon mot about the occasion representing the greatest gathering of minds at the White House since "Thomas Jefferson dined here alone." The Nobelists roared their appreciation at this elegant bouquet, and I sensed the words passing into immortality.

The White House was anything but smoke-free, and the scullions among us lit up our cigarettes. I noticed with my usual sulkiness and envy that many gentlemen at the tables around the room had begun to smoke cigars; among them was Kennedy, who was engaged in conversation with a stunning golden-haired young woman and plainly relishing her at least as much as his Churchill. Following coffee, we moved into the East Room for a concert of chamber music; after this, just as the party was breaking up and we were about to be converted into pumpkins, I was astonished to learn from an army captain in full dress that Rose and I were invited upstairs for something "more intimate" with President and Mrs. Kennedy. Although I had an instant's impish fantasy about what the "more intimate" implied—this was, after all, the dawn of the Swinging 60s—I was in fact rather relieved to discover that the small room into which we were ushered was filled with cigar smokers and their lady companions.

The president hadn't arrived yet, but

Styron's revisions to the Vanity Fair *proofs of "Havanas in Camelot."*

ished to learn from an army captain in full dress that Rose and I were invited upstairs for something "more intimate" with President and Mrs. Kennedy. Although I had an instant's impish fantasy about what "more intimate" implied—this was, after all, the dawn of the Swinging Sixties—I was in fact rather relieved to discover that the small room into which we were ushered was filled with cigar smokers and their lady companions.

The president hadn't arrived yet, but Jackie was there, as were Goodwin and Schlesinger and Bobby Kennedy and Pierre Salinger, together with their wives, and all the men were focusing on their Havanas with such obvious pleasure that one might have thought the entire Nobel dinner had been arranged to produce this fragrant climax. Only in fine Paris restaurants, where—unlike in America—cigar smoking was encouraged, had I inhaled such a delicious aroma. I had by this time taken aboard too many of the various beverages the White House had provided, including the dessert champagne (Piper-Heidsieck 1955), and sank down unwittingly into the president's famous rocking chair.

Rocking away, I talked with Lionel Trilling, the renowned critic; he and his wife, Diana, were the only other literary people invited upstairs. He was also the only other cigarette smoker, as far as I could tell—indeed, a real chain-smoker, with a haggard, oxygen-deprived look—

and we made book chat and indulged in our forlorn habit while the others convivially enjoyed their great cigars. It was not until Schlesinger discreetly asked me to let the president sit down in the rocker, for the sake of his dysfunctional back, that I realized that J.F.K. had been standing in the room for some time, too polite to shoo me out of his chair. When I leapt up, mortified, and Kennedy apologetically took my place, I noticed that he was still fondling his Churchill. The leader of the Free World wreathed in smoke, gently rocking: this was the relaxed and contented image I took away with me when, well after midnight, we wobbled our way homeward from one hell of a party.

IN THE MONTHS THAT intervened before I saw Kennedy again, I waged a demonic struggle with my cigarette habit. Thanks to my two White House gurus, I was also gingerly experimenting with cigars. The embargo against Cuba, instituted officially by Kennedy himself, was now in force; Havanas had become nearly unavailable overnight, and so I found myself buying the next-best cigars, which were then being made in the Canary Islands. These cigars were actually very good, and many of them were outstanding.

But I was still hesitant to commit myself. Although I was fully aware that I was undermining my health with an addiction that had held me captive since the age of fifteen,

I was unable to make the transition to cigars without going through convulsions of moral doubt. Actually, I was a victim of the conventional wisdom. This was because in America, an essentially puritanical society that is as absolutist in its views about health as it is about many other issues, there was little distinction to be made between cigarettes and cigars.

After all, in a country which some years later, in its panic over the cholesterol in eggs, would virtually banish this agelessly invaluable food from the national diet rather than merely caution moderation, it was entirely natural that the relatively harmless pleasure of moderate cigar smoking should suffer the same opprobrium as the lethal addiction to cigarettes. If I stopped cigarettes, there were a lot of old nannies of both sexes eager to tell me: cigars are just as bad!

Well, they plainly are not, and indeed, unlike cigarettes, they possess an intrinsic good. At that time, in notes I made for a 1963 review (in the *New York Review of Books*) of *The Consumers Union Report on Smoking and the Public Interest*, which was a precursor to the original surgeon general's report on the hazards of tobacco, I wrote:

> It is a grim irony that in our health-obsessed society an addiction as plainly ruinous as cigarette smoking should be condoned and promoted while the com-

paratively benign use of cigars should be condemned as if it were a plague. Cigars are a genuine
pleasure; cigarettes are a pseudo-pleasure, of the
same kind experienced by laboratory rats. The
stigma against cigars has as much to do with eco-
nomics and social class as it has with misplaced
moralizing. The nearly universal habit of cigarette
smoking is the property of the vast middle class,
while cigar smokers are confined to the upper and
lower ends of the economic scale. (There are over-
lappings and intersections, of course, but this is the
basic contour.)

Among middle-class cigarette smokers, cigars
are regarded either as the overpriced indulgence of
bankers, rich corporate board members, and movie
moguls like Darryl Zanuck or, at the lower end, the
cheap habit of White Owl chompers who inhabit
low-class saloons and sleazy gyms. The comic-strip
figure of the 1930s "Pete the Tramp" best illustrates
this dichotomy: the little drifter always on the look-
out for plutocrats' quality cigar butts, which he'd
pluck from the gutter and impale on a toothpick.

Cigars have never found a comfortable middle
ground of acceptance. What compounds the irony
is that White Owls and Dutch Masters do in fact offend the nostrils—certainly mine—and women,

especially, with their canary-like sensitivity, are often justifiably upset by such effluvia. Women disturbed by cheap mass-produced cigars have innocently helped give all cigars a bum rap. What is so fascinating is that the same women, when exposed to the smoke of a prime Montecristo, will often emit genuine swooning sounds, thus demonstrating that cigars of high quality need not endure prejudice forever. Women someday will be smoking cigars. I predict, too, that at some point in the future, after society has become aware of the awful hazards of cigarettes, many of the middle class will begin gradually to embrace cigars—cigars of excellence which, coming from countries other than Cuba, will also become more and more affordable.

I'm pleased to find that my crystal ball, so often dismally clouded, was quite clear when I set down those last lines.

THE FOLLOWING SUMMER I quit smoking cigarettes for good, cold turkey. It was just a few weeks before Jack Kennedy invited Rose and me out for a ride on his cabin cruiser, the good ship *Patrick J*. He and Jackie crossed over from the Cape to Martha's Vineyard, where I had rented a house, and took us out on an overcast August day for a wallowing luncheon afloat. Aside from my friends John and Sue Marquand, who accompanied us, the only other passenger aboard was the late Stephen Smith, J.F.K.'s brother-in-law. A Coast Guard cutter hung around not far away for security reasons, but otherwise the seven of us had the rolling waves to ourselves. The sea was moderately rough, though alcohol soothed the mal de mer. The Bloody Marys, poured out by a rather jittery Filipino mess steward, overflowed their glasses; there was a lot of chitchat between the Marquands and Jack and Jackie, who had known each other for years, about mutual friends; variations on the twist, and other hip music of that year, blared from a record player; and the general pre-luncheon mood was frisky despite the gray weather.

The talk became a little bit more serious when we sat down to eat. At the table of the *Patrick J*'s open cockpit, no one paid much attention to the disastrous lunch. It was a mad joke of cold hot dogs in soggy buns, gooey *oeufs en gelée*, spoons dropped by the nervous Filipino into everyone's laps, glasses of beer not merely iced but frozen solid. We got involved instead in the conversation, which ranged from Massachusetts politics and the racial situation heating up in the Deep South—the previous fall's violent events in Oxford, Mississippi, had plainly shaken J.F.K.— to the old chestnut about whether Alger Hiss was guilty

(Kennedy thought he was) and the president's obvious pique over an article in the *American Scholar* by the critic Alfred Kazin questioning his intellectual credentials. I was both amused and impressed that Kazin should bug him so.

A lot of the time Jackie kept her shapely but rather large bare feet in the presidential lap. At one point J.F.K., in a personal aside to me, asked what I was writing, and when I told him it was a novel about Nat Turner, who had led a nineteenth-century slave insurrection in Virginia, he became immediately alert and probed me brightly and persistently for information, which I was happy to provide. He seemed fascinated by my story of the revolt. The issue of race was plainly beginning to bedevil Kennedy, as it was nearly everyone else. At that time few Americans had heard of Nat Turner. I told Kennedy things about slavery he had obviously never known before.

Then, after the ice cream and coffee, the president passed out to the men Partagas cigars, made in Havana and encased in silver tubes. I rolled mine around between my fingers delightedly, trying not to crack too obvious a smile. I was aware that this was a contraband item under the embargo against Cuban goods and that the embargo had been promulgated by the very man who had just pressed the cigar into my hand. Therefore the Partagas was all the more worth preserving, at least for a while, in its protective tube, as a naughty memento, a conversation piece with a touch of scandal. I watched as the president began to smoke with pleasure, displaying no sense of the clandestine. I palmed the Partagas into my pocket while Kennedy wasn't looking, resolved to smoke it on some special occasion, and lit up one of my Canary Island coronas. Soon afterward, however, I began feeling a certain odd, fugitive sadness at this little gift from Kennedy, a sadness I couldn't quite fathom, though it may have been only the same poignant regret that prompted me to write, later on, when I remembered the boat trip, "of the irreconcilable differences, the ferocious animosity that separated Castro and Kennedy. Of all the world's leaders the Harvard man and the Marxist from Havana were temperamentally and intellectually most alike, they probably would have taken warmly to each other had not the storm of twentieth-century history and its bizarre determinism made them into unshakable enemies."

I saw Kennedy again the following November at a crowded, elegant party one Friday night in New York. I'd thought, before going, that we might get a brief glimpse of him and nothing more. But Rose and I, entering the dinner, discovered him at the bottom of a flight of stairs looking momentarily lost and abandoned. As if arrested in an instant's solitude, he was talking to no one and pondering his cigar. He had a splendid Palm Beach tan. He threw his arms around us and uttered a line so cornily ingratiating that it gave blarney new meaning: "How did they get *you* to come here? They had a hard enough time getting me!" He asked me how the novel was coming, and once again he began to talk about race. Did I know any Negro writers? Could I suggest some Negro names for a meeting at the White House? And so on. Finally someone distracted him and he disappeared into the crowd. Sometime later, on his way out, he caught my eye and, smiling, said, "Take care."

They were words I should have spoken to him, for exactly two weeks later, on another Friday, he was dead in Dallas.

I smoked the Partagas in his memory.

—*Vanity Fair*, JULY 1996

A CASE OF
THE GREAT POX

AMONG THE PERFORMANCES THAT HELPED MAKE
the movie *Casablanca* immortal was that of Claude Rains
as the French police captain Louis Renault. Rains played
the part with astringent urbanity and created a lasting
model of the tough cop attractively humanized, Monsieur
Nice Guy lurking behind the domineering swaggerer. I
belong to the first of several generations that have fallen
under the film's febrile romantic spell. By the late autumn
of 1944 I had seen the film three times, and Rains seemed
to me only slightly less crucial to its hypnotic unfolding
than Bogart and Bergman. You may well imagine my
amazement, then, when, in that wartime autumn, a verita-
ble replica—the spitting image—of Claude Rains sat behind a desk in a doctor's office on the urological ward of
the naval hospital at Parris Island, South Carolina. I stood
at attention, looking down at him. A sign on the desk identified the doctor as "B. Klotz, Lieutenant Commander,

Chief of Urology." I recall registering all sorts of impressions at once: the name Klotz, with its pathological overtone, and Klotz-Rains himself, duplicated—somewhat narcissistically, I thought—as he posed in prewar civvies in one of several framed photographs on the wall. The other photographs, completing a kind of triumvirate of authority, were of President Franklin D. Roosevelt and Admiral Ernest J. King, chief of naval operations. There was one notable difference between Klotz and Rains, aside from the doctor's white blouse instead of the gendarmerie kepi and tunic. It was that the actor, even when he was trying to be threatening, had a twinkly charm, a barely repressed bonhomie, while Klotz appeared merely threatening. I knew that this was not the beginning of a beautiful friendship. That morning, Klotz sat silent for a moment, then came directly to the point. No elegant British vocables. In a flat, mid-Atlantic accent, he said, "Your blood tests have been checked out, and they indicate that you have syphilis."

I remember my cheeks and the region around my mouth going numb, then beginning to tingle, as if my face had been dealt a brutal whack. Traumatic events powerfully focus the perceptions, leaving ancillary details embalmed forever in memory—in this case, the window just beyond Klotz's head, a frost-rimed pane through which I could see the vast asphalt parade ground swarming with platoon after platoon of marine recruits like me (or like me until the day before, when I was sent to the hospital), performing the rigorous choreography of close-order drill. Dawn had not yet broken, and the men moved in and out of the light that fell in bright pools from the barracks. Most of the platoons were marching with rifles, a drill instructor tramping alongside and screaming orders that I couldn't hear but that, up close, would have sounded like those of a foul-mouthed and hysterical madman. Other platoons remained still, at ease, shrouded in cigarette smoke or exhaled breath or both; it was a bitterly cold November. Beyond the parade ground and its clumps of marines in green field jackets were rows of wooden barracks. And beyond the barracks lay the waters of Port Royal Sound, roiled by an icy wind. All these things registered in my mind clearly, but at the same time they seemed to coalesce around a single word, uttered by the voice of Klotz: *syphilis*.

"You will remain on this ward indefinitely for further observation," Klotz continued. There was an unmistakably antagonistic tone in his voice. Most doctors in my past—the few I'd had contact with, anyway—had been chummy, avuncular, and genuinely if sometimes clumsily sweet-mannered. Klotz was of another breed, and he caused my stomach to go into spasm. I thought, What a prick. Before dismissing me, he ordered me to report to the duty pharmacist's mate, who would instruct me about the series of regulations I'd be subject to while on the ward, a regime Klotz referred to as "the venereal protocol." He then told me to return to my bed, where I would wait until further notice. I was wearing a blue hospital robe, in the pocket of which I had thrust a copy of one of the first paperback anthologies ever published, a volume that had kept me company for at least two years—*The Pocket Book of Verse*, compiled by an academic named M. Edmund Speare. My legs had an aqueous, flimsy feeling. I lurched back down the ward, still numb around the mouth, gripping the book with feverish desire, like a condemned Christian clutching a Testament.

I SHOULD SAY A WORD about the great pox, so named, in the sixteenth century, to distinguish the illness from smallpox. Although syphilis had been regarded, since the late fifteenth century, as a plague that would never in any real sense yield to the strategies of medical science, it had been dealt a sudden and mortal blow only a year or so before my diagnosis. It was one of medicine's most dramatic victories, like Jenner's discovery of a smallpox vaccine or Pasteur's defeat of rabies. The breakthrough took place soon after American researchers—building on the work of Sir Alexander Fleming, who had discovered penicillin, in the twenties, and Sir Howard Florey, who had developed a technique for producing the drug—found that a one-week course of the miraculous mold could wipe out all traces of early syphilis, and even certain late-stage manifestations of the illness. (Penicillin also had a devastating effect on the other major venereal scourge, gonorrhea, a single injection usually being sufficient to put it to rout.) Since mid-1943, the medical authorities of the American armed forces had ordered doctors in military hospitals around the globe to discontinue a syphilis treatment called arsphenamine therapy and to commence using penicillin as it became available. Arsphenamine—better known, variously, as Salvarsan, 606, or the magic bullet—was an arsenic-based compound developed in 1909 by the German bacteriologist Paul Ehrlich. He discovered that his new drug (the six hundred and sixth version proved successful) could knock out syphilis without killing the patient; it was a remarkable advance after several hundred years during which the principal nostrum was mercury, a substance that worked capriciously, when it worked at all, and was for the most part as dangerous as the disease itself.

Because the disease sprang from the dark act of sex, *syphilis* was not a word uttered casually in the Protestant environment of my Virginia boyhood; the word raised eyebrows around America even when it was discreetly murmured in *Dr. Ehrlich's Magic Bullet*, a 1940 movie starring Edward G. Robinson, who I thought was a pretty convincing healer after his parts as a ruthless mobster. *Dr. Ehrlich's Magic Bullet* didn't make much of an impression on me; I doubtless was too young. But even if I had been older I would probably not have realized that the movie failed to tell an essential truth. While the doctor's magic bullet was a vast improvement over the forlorn remedy of the past, his treatment was shown to be sadly insufficient; the drug rendered patients noncontagious, but it wasn't a very reliable cure, and the treatment required dozens of painful and costly injections over such a long period of time—often many months—that a great number of patients became discouraged, and were consequently prone to relapses. So the epidemic suffered a setback but was not halted. It would take Alexander Fleming's surefire bactericidal fungus to produce the real magic. And I was in the vanguard of those victims upon whom this benison would descend. Or so it seemed, until, with a gradual dawning that was sickening in itself, I began to suspect that health was not so readily at hand.

As a diagnosed syphilitic, I had good cause to think passionately about penicillin during the interminable hours and days I spent in the Clap Shack, as such wards were known throughout the navy. But, from the first day following Dr. Klotz's announcement, I had the impression that I was a very special case. I was not an ordinary patient whose treatment would follow the uneventful trajectory toward cure, but one who had been hurled into an incomprehensible purgatory where neither treatment nor even the possibility of a cure was part of my ultimate destiny. And this hunch turned out to be correct. From the outset, I was convinced not only that I had acquired the most feared of sexually transmitted diseases but that I would at some point keel over from it, probably in an unspeakable cellular mud slide or convulsion of the nervous system. As an early-blooming hypochondriac, a reader besotted with *The Merck Manual*, I had a bit more medical savvy than most kids my age, and what my diagnosis actually portended made me clammy with dismay. I believed that I was beyond the reach of penicillin. I was sure that I was a goner, and that certainty never left me during the days that stretched into weeks of weirdly demoralizing confinement.

My bed was at the very end of the ward, and I had a view from two windows, at right angles to each other. From one window, I could see the sound, a shallow inlet of the Atlantic, on the edge of freezing; from the other, I had a glimpse of a row of barracks not far away and, between the barrack buildings, concrete laundry slabs, where marines bedeviled by the cold—I watched them shake and shiver—pounded at their near-frozen dungarees beneath sluiceways of water. What nasty little Schadenfreude I might have felt at their plight was dispelled by my own despair at having been separated from longtime buddies whom I'd gone to college with, officer candidates like me—or like the person I had been before the onset of an illness that, because of its carnal origin and the moral shame it entailed, would prevent me from even thinking of becoming a lieutenant in the United States Marine Corps.

Winkler, the hospital corpsman who had checked me onto the ward, returned to bring me these tidings. No way, he said, that you can get a marine commission if you've had V.D. He had other awful news, too, most of it bearing on my health. After escorting me to my sack and telling me where to stow my seabag, he told me—in answer to my bewildered "Why the hell am I here?"—that my Kahn test was so high it had gone off the chart. "It looks to me," he said with maddening whimsy, "like you've got a case of the great pox." When I asked him what a Kahn test was, he replied with a counterquestion: Had I ever heard of a Wassermann reaction? I replied, Of course, every schoolboy knew about a Wassermann. A Kahn, Winkler explained, was almost the same as a Wassermann, only an improvement. It was a simpler blood test. And then, as I recalled the endless trips I'd made in past days to the regimental dispensary to verify the first routine test, and the vial after vial of blood extracted from my arm, I had a foreshadowing of the stern warrant that Dr. Klotz would serve up to me the following morning. I must have radiated terror, for I sensed a conscious effort by Winkler to make me feel better; his tactic was to try to cast me as one of the elite. At the moment, he told me, I was the only syphilitic on the ward. Most of the patients were guys with the clap. And when, despondently, I asked him why he thought victims of syphilis, as opposed to those with gonorrhea, were such rarities, he came back with a theory that in my case was so richly inconceivable that it caused me to laugh one of the last spontaneous laughs I would laugh for a long time. "You can catch the clap a lot easier than syphilis," he explained. "Syph you really have to work at to contract." He added, with a hint of admiration, "You must have been getting a new piece of ass every day."

After my interview with Klotz, which took place very early, before his regular morning rounds, I had a chance to sit next to my bed and take stock of my situation while the other patients slept. Winkler had explained the configuration of the ward. It was a warehouse of genitourinary complaints. On one side of the ward were a dozen beds occupied by clap patients. As a result of crowding in the clap section, I was lodged on the other side of the center aisle, at the end of a row of patients whose maladies were not venereal in origin. Most of these marines had kidney and bladder disorders, primarily infections; there was a boy who had suffered a serious blow to his kidney during one of the savage internecine boxing matches that the drill instructors, virtually all sadists, enjoyed promoting during morning exercises. There was an undescended testicle that Winkler said would never have got past the first medical screening in the robust volunteer days, before the draft allowed all sorts of misshapen characters into the Marine Corps. The marine in the sack next to me, breathing softly, his face expressionless in sleep's bland erasure, had just the day before been circumcised by Dr. Klotz; the fellow had suffered from a constrictive condition of the foreskin known as phimosis. Winkler's last task the previous night had been to swaddle the guy's groin in ice packs, lest nocturnal erections rip out the stitches—a mishap that obviously could never happen to a Jew, said Winkler, who was plainly New York Jewish, in a tone that was a touch self-satisfied. As for the marines with the clap, Winkler pointed out that in most cases this was not your standard garden-variety gonorrhea but an intractable chronic condition that usually came about as a result of the guys' refusing, out of shame or fear—and often out of sheer indifference—to seek treatment, so that the invasive gonococci began after time to wreak havoc in the prostate, or became lodged in the joints as an exquisitely painful form of arthritis. Marines and sailors from up and down the Atlantic coast came to this ward for what was possibly last-ditch therapy, since Klotz was known as the best doctor in the navy for handling such complications.

Later that first day, another hospital corpsman outlined to me the details of the venereal protocol. V.D. patients were in certain respects strictly segregated, both from their fellow sufferers on the ward and from the hospital population at large. Our robes were emblazoned with a large yellow V over the breast. When we went to the head, we were expected to use specially designated toilets and basins. Those of us who were ambulatory were to eat at mess-hall tables reserved for our use. When we attended the twice-weekly movies at the base recreation center, we would be escorted in a separate group and then seated together in a section marked off by a yellow ribbon. I remember absorbing this information with queasiness, and then asking the corpsman why we were subject to such extraordinary precautions. While I was not unaware of the perils of V.D., I had no idea that we posed such a threat. But as soon as I began to express my puzzlement, the corpsman explained that syphilis and gonorrhea were contagious as hell. True, most people got them only from sex, but one of those little microorganisms could infect through a tiny scratch. BUMED (as the Bureau of Medicine was called) was taking no chances; furthermore, he added with a knowing look, Dr. Klotz "had a kind of personal fixation." This was an enigmatic, faintly sinister statement that became less opaque as time passed and Klotz became the dominant presence in my life.

As the only patient with syphilis, I was spared the short-arm inspection that was the centerpiece of Dr. Klotz's early rounds that morning and every morning at the stroke of six. At that hour, a bell in the ward jangled and the overhead lights came on in an explosion. The bedridden on my side of the aisle remained in their sacks. But in the interval of a minute or so between the flood of light and the appearance of Dr. Klotz, the dozen clap patients in the opposite row all scrambled to their feet and stood at ragged attention. There was usually a certain amount of wisecracking among these guys, along with self-dramatizing groans and reciprocal "Fuck you's." Most of them were regulars, not effete college-bred recruits like me, and were five or ten years older than me. Their accents were about equally divided between southern cracker and northeastern working class. I soon understood that many of these die-hard cases had one thing in common: they were obsessive Romeos, fornicators of serene dedication whose commitment to sexual bliss was so wholehearted that they could keep up a flow of jokes even as the disease that such pleasure had cost them gnawed away at the inmost mucous membranes of the genitalia and tortured the joints of their wrists and knees.

I was amazed at this nonchalance, and also at their apparently incandescent libidos, especially since my own nineteen-year-old hormonal heat had plunged to absolute zero the instant Dr. Klotz confirmed the nature of my problem; the word *syphilis* had made the very notion of sex nauseating, as if I were beset by some erotic anorexia. But the members of the gonorrhea faction quieted down as soon as Winkler or one of the other corpsmen shouted, "Attention on deck!" and Klotz made his businesslike entrance through the swinging doors. It was important, Winkler had told me, that these bums be inspected as soon as they woke up, before heading to the urinals; from looking at the accumulated purulence called gleet, and checking the amount and consistency of the discharge, Klotz could determine how the treatment was proceeding. And so, accompanied by a litany—"Skin it back, squeeze it, milk it down"—intoned by the corpsman, Klotz would pass down the line of victims, making his evaluations. He didn't waste a word, and his manner was frostily judgmental, as if these rogues and whoremongers were unworthy of even so much as a casual "Good morning." Nor was his manner with me any less reproachful. As I stood stiffly at attention, I was thankful only that I didn't have to submit my dick to such a degrading scrutiny at that hour of the morning. During each tour of the ward, Klotz would glare at me briefly, ask the corpsman about my daily Kahn test—it remained at the highest (and therefore the most alarming) level, day in and day out—and then pass on to the nonvenereal patients.

Early in the afternoon on that first day, however, Klotz did examine my penis. This was a procedure that I might ordinarily skip describing were it not for the monstrous effect that it had on my psychic balance, which had already been thrown badly out of whack. For it was Klotz's judgment regarding my penile history that helped crystallize my belief that I was doomed. I was summoned to his office, and, as I stood in front of him, he checked through my medical-record book and brusquely asked some routine questions. Any history of syphilis in my family? (What a question!) No, I lied. In the preceding weeks or months had I experienced any unusual rash or fever? I had not. Any swelling in the groin? No. Had I noticed any unusual growth on my penis? This would be a hard, painless ulcer, he said, called a chancre. I knew what a chancre was, everyone had heard about chancres (corpsmen were even known as "chancre mechanics"); but I had not seen one. During Klotz's interrogation, I held in view the eye-level portrait of a solemn, resolute Franklin D. Roosevelt, who kept looking back at me. I was grateful for the reassuring gaze of this surrogate father, my perennial president, the only one I had ever known, and I steadfastly stared back at him through most of Klotz's examination, which he carried out with cold, skeletal fingers.

He twisted my penis, not very gently, gave it an unnecessary squeeze or two, and turned it upside down. I recall thinking that, though it had known various attitudes, it had rarely been upside down. Then he bade me to look down, saying that he had discovered, on the underside, a scar. Chancres leave scars, he murmured, and this looked like a chancre scar. I glanced down and, indeed, discerned a scar. A tiny reddish outcropping. Since the chancre had been painless, he added, it had come and gone, without my ever noticing its presence, leaving only that small scar. He seemed to have put aside, at least for the moment, his customary distaste. He said that the chance of my having been infected by nonvenereal contact was astronomically remote. The toilet seat was a myth. Syphilis usually created distinct symptoms, he went on—first the chancre, then, later, the fever and the rash—but quite often these symptoms never appeared, or appeared so insubstantially that they went unnoticed. Klotz surprised me by saying something that, in the midst of his dispassionate exegesis, sounded almost poetic: "Syphilis is a cruel disease." And then, after a brief silence, during which I became aware that he was constructing an answer to the question that sheer fright kept me from asking, he declared, "What happens in the end is that syphilis invades the rest of the body." He paused and concluded, before dismissing me, "We're going to have to keep you here and figure out just how far it's advanced."

I went back to my bed at the end of the ward and, in the

cold midday light, lay down. You weren't supposed to lie on a bed in daytime, but I did anyway. The hospital was a venerable wooden structure, warm, even overheated, but I felt nearly frozen, listening to the windows creaking and banging in the bluster of an Atlantic gale. The sex maniacs with the clap across the aisle were noisily trading lewd adventures, and I gradually sank into a stupor of disbelief, beyond the consoling power of even *The Pocket Book of Verse*, which had saved me in many a lesser crisis but was plainly beyond the scope of this one.

ITS HISTORY "IS UNIQUE AMONG GREAT DISEASES," the medical historian William Allen Pusey wrote, "in that it does not gradually emerge into the records of medicine as its character becomes recognized, but appears on the stage of history with a dramatic suddenness in keeping with the tragic reputation it has made; as a great plague sweeping within a few years over the known world."

This observation, made in the early part of the century, has an all too painful resonance today, and it might be worthwhile to compare syphilis with our present pandemic. Unlike AIDS, syphilis was not invariably fatal, despite its extremely high rate of mortality. This may have been its only saving grace, depending on whether death is viewed as a blessing preferable to the terrible and irreversible damage the disease is capable of inflicting on the body and the mind. After the introduction of Dr. Ehrlich's not-so-magic bullet, and especially after penicillin's knock-out blow, syphilis lost much of its capacity to evoke universal dread. Still, for various reasons, it remained a horror, aside from the fact that no one wants to be infested by millions of *Treponema pallidum*, the causative microbe, whose wriggling corkscrew can reach the bone marrow and spleen within forty-eight hours of infection, and produce a persistent malaise, rashes, ulcerous skin lesions, and other debilitating symptoms. For one thing, there was the stigma—and I mean the appalling stigma arising from anything at all suggesting misbehavior as we young people traversed the parched sexual landscape of the thirties and forties.

I've mentioned that the word itself was taboo. Among nice people, *syphilis* was uttered sotto voce if at all, and only occasionally found its way into print. *Social disease* and *vice disease* were the usual substitutes. When I was in grade school, the only time I recall the word's catching my eye was when I happened upon it in a medical pamphlet. I asked my teacher, a maiden lady of traditional reserve, what it meant. She instantly corrected my pronunciation, but her cheeks became flushed, and she didn't answer my question. Her silence made me guess at something wicked. And wicked it was in those prim years. For most of its existence in the Anglo-Saxon world, syphilis, as AIDS has often done, stained the people who contracted it with indelible disrepute.

But there was a far graver trouble: the sheer awfulness of the malady itself. Even after medical intervention, and treatment with penicillin, there could still be dire complications. No cure was absolutely foolproof. And my obsession—that syphilis had taken possession of my system and had commenced its inroads, penetrating tissues and organs, which thus had already suffered the first effects of dissolution—grew more fixed every day as I dragged myself through Dr. Klotz's venereal protocol. I wore my yellow V stoically, and soon got used to going to the mess hall and the movies in a segregated herd. I had plenty of time to brood about my condition, since there were no organized activities for patients on the ward. I kept wondering why I was not being treated. If penicillin could work its miracle, why was it not being used? It only aggravated my distress to think that the disease, for reasons beyond my understanding, had reached a stage where treatment was useless, and was merely waiting for some fatal resolution. I had to blot out thoughts like these. Mostly, I hung around the area near my bed, sitting on a camp stool and reading books and magazines from the small hospital library. I returned hesitantly to *The Pocket*

Book of Verse, to Keats and A. E. Housman and Emily Dickinson and *The Rubáiyát of Omar Khayyám*.

Except during morning rounds, I never saw Dr. Klotz. My only actual duty was to bare my arm once a day for the Kahn test, which invariably showed the same results: "Off the chart," as Winkler had said. I grew friendly with Winkler, who seemed drawn to me, most likely because I'd been to college and he'd had two years at CCNY before Pearl Harbor. One of his generosities was a loan of a little red Motorola portable radio, which I kept tuned to the Savannah station and its news about the war. The bulletins added weight to the black and anxious mood that each afternoon crept over me—a mood that I would recognize only years later as the onset of a serious depression.

Just before I entered the hospital, marines had stormed ashore on a remote Pacific island called Peleliu and had met with "heavy Japanese resistance"—a common Pentagon euphemism to describe our troops' being slaughtered. What I heard on the radio was unsettling enough, but the news chiefly reminded me of the doubtfulness of my own future. For at least three years, I had lived with the bold and heady ambition of becoming a marine lieutenant; to lead troops into combat against the Japs had been an intoxicating dream. A sexually transmitted disease was not permissible for an officer candidate, Winkler had ruefully pointed out to me—not even if he was cured, so ugly was the moral blotch—and thus I began to realize that the microorganisms seething like termites within me were destroying my vision of honor and achievement as effectively as they were laying waste to my flesh. But this regret, wrenching as it was, I could somehow deal with. What was close to intolerable—beyond the disgrace, beyond the wreckage it would make of my military ambition—was the premonition, settling around me like a fog bank, of absolute physical ruin. A death-in-life, for example, like that of my Uncle Harold, whose case was a harrowing paradigm of the malady and the disaster it could inflict.

He was my mother's younger brother, and at twenty-seven, during the Great War, he had gone overseas as an infantry corporal in the Rainbow Division. During the Saint-Mihiel offensive, he had suffered a bad shrapnel wound in the leg and had been mustered out in 1918 to his hometown, in western Pennsylvania, where he married, had a son, and settled down to the life of a businessman. Sometime in the late twenties, he started to display odd behavioral symptoms: he woke at night in the grip of nightmares, and began to have terrifying hallucinations. He complained of anxiety and had almost daily episodes of feverish agitation, which caused him to speak of suicide. He told anyone who would listen that he was tormented by memories of the war, the agony of men and animals, the carnage. After he disappeared for a week and was finally found in a dingy Pittsburgh hotel room, fifty miles away, his wife made him seek medical help. At a veterans-aid clinic a diagnosis was made of extreme psychosis as a result of the violence of war. The syndrome in those years was generally known as "shell shock." My uncle was sent to the mental unit of the veterans hospital in Perry Point, Maryland, and there he remained for the rest of his life.

I recall visiting Uncle Harold with my mother and father once when I was a young boy, before the war. We were going to New York, and the visit was planned as a side trip on our way from Virginia. I had never seen him, except as a figure in photographs taken years earlier: a cheery kid with prominent teeth, like my mother's, and flashing, exuberant eyes. I had been fascinated by Uncle Harold, the war hero, and he had taken on for me an almost mythic shape. My mother was devoted to him, and, as a sedulous eavesdropper, I couldn't help but absorb all the captivating details of his dramatic life: the flaming battle for Saint-Mihiel that killed more than four thousand Americans, his letters describing the savagery of combat, his painful recovery in a convalescent facility behind the front, the breakdown in Pennsylvania, his sad confinement. By the time we turned up at the veterans hospital on a luminous June day, I was looking forward excitedly, though with a touch of squirmy disquiet, to meeting my shell-shocked uncle. I don't remember whether my parents prepared me for the encounter, but it was certainly not like anything I might have imagined, and I think that they, too, may not have been ready for such an apparition.

The male attendant who brought him outside to greet us on the lawn seemed to feel the need to urge him along, as he tottered toward us in his army-issue robe and slippers, with gentle but persistent prods to the back. This probably made him look even more helpless and disoriented than he actually was, but he was plainly a soul without a mooring. I was alarmed by his shambling gait and his empty gaze; I couldn't reconcile the old face, so bony and desiccated, and the balding skull and trembling hands with the vivid boy of the pictures. Most awful to me was the moment when he mechanically embraced my mother and whispered, "Hello, Edith." It was the name of their older sister.

We remained there on the hospital lawn for perhaps no more than an hour, amid the debris of a messy picnic. Uncle Harold said almost nothing as we sat on a bench, and the monosyllables my mother coaxed from him had a softly gargled incoherence. I knew that this was a scene I couldn't continue to witness, and I turned away in misery from my uncle and his drowned, sweetly musing brown eyes, and from the sight of my mother clutching his palsied hand, squeezing it over and over in some hopeless attempt at comfort or connection.

I later learned the truth about Uncle Harold. My father did not tell me until several years after my mother died, when I was eighteen or so, and presumably old enough to absorb the dread secret that our kinsman had been suffering not from shell shock but from syphilis. My father was a candid and sophisticated man, but even he had an awkward time telling me the truth. After the shock wore off, the knowledge that my uncle was still alive—that, as was so often the case, the microbes, rather than quickly murdering their host, held him hostage while they continued their leisurely depredations—made me ache inside. The great pox could dwell in a body for decades. By the time he was sent to the veterans hospital he was most likely afflicted by late syphilis; according to my father, the disease was acquired after his marriage and the birth of his only child. There was never a hint that either my aunt or my cousin, a boy whom I spent many summers with, had been tainted by the illness. But who knew exactly when he had got it? Somehow the plague had entered him. It had been a quiet case, but viciously malignant, beyond reach of the magic bullet or any other medical stratagem, and at the time of our visit he was succumbing to forms of neurosyphilis that devastate the brain and the spinal cord. The spirochetes had wrought a vegetative madness.

I thought a lot about Uncle Harold during my stay on the ward. Especially at night, in the dark, with Winkler's little radio pressed against my ear, trying to distract myself with the Artie Shaw or Glenn Miller tunes I could capture from the other, I'd have a moment of sudden, heart-stopping panic and my uncle would draw ineluctably near. I could sense him in his hospital robe, silent, standing somewhere close by among the sleeping marines, a stooped figure whose presence portended a future I dared not think about.

WHILE ON A TRIP THROUGH EUROPE in 1760, Giovanni Casanova, that tireless gadabout, cocksman, and celebrity hound, stopped at Ferney to pay a visit to Voltaire. There seems to be no record of the two superstars' talking about syphilis, but it would have been a fitting topic, given its perennial fashionableness, and if they had spoken of it their attitude, in all likelihood, would have had a mocking overtone. Voltaire never let the horrid nature of the illness obtrude upon his own lighthearted view of it—he wrote wittily about the great pox in *Candide*—and throughout Casanova's memoirs there are anecdotes about syphilis that the author plainly regards as excruciatingly funny. Making sport of it may have been the only way in which the offspring of the Enlightenment could come to grips with a pestilence that seemed as immutably fixed in history as war or famine. In a secular age, gags were appropriate for an inexplicable calamity that in olden times had been regarded as divine retribution. Previous centuries had seen people calling on God for help, and God had not answered.

The disease first swept like a hurricane over Europe during the period of Columbus's voyages (whether Columbus and his crew were responsible for importing syphilis from the West Indies is disputed by scholars, but it seems a strong possibility), and it took an exceptionally virulent form, often killing its victims in the secondary, or rash-and-fever, stage, which most people in later epochs (including me) weathered without harm. In its congenital mode, it was particularly disfiguring and malevolent, which increased the terror. No wonder that the Diet of Worms, the same assembly that condemned Martin Luther for heresy, issued a mandate declaring that the "evil pocks" was a scourge visited upon mankind for the sin of blasphemy.

But it was the doctrine of original sin, falling upon both Catholics and backslid Presbyterians like me, that made the sufferers of syphilis pay a special price in moral blame unknown to those who acquired other diseases. This was particularly true in the early Victorian era, when a return to faith, after a long time of frivolous impiety, was coupled with a return to the Pauline precept that the act of sex is an act of badness—absolute badness more often than not, exceeding all other abominations. This connection with sexuality gave syphilis, in a puritanical culture, its peculiar aura of degradation. As Susan Sontag has shown in *Illness as Metaphor,* her study of the mythology of disease, all the major illnesses have prompted a moralistic and punitive response, and have given rise to entire theoretical systems based on phony psychologizing. The bubonic plague implied widespread moral pollution; tuberculosis was the product of thwarted passion and blighted hopes, or sprang from "defective vitality, or vitality misspent"; out of emotional frustration or repression of feeling has come the curse of cancer, whose victims are also often demonically possessed. As I have discovered firsthand, mental disorders may be the worst, inviting suspicion of inborn feebleness. In such views, the disease itself expresses the character of the victim. Syphilis, however, has suffered a different stigma, one that has been of a singularly repellent sort. It has reflected neither feebleness nor misspent vitality nor repression of feeling—only moral squalor. In recent years, AIDS has been similarly stigmatized, despite extensive enlightenment. But in square, churchgoing America at the time of my diagnosis, a syphilitic was regarded not as a sexual hobbyist whose pastime had got out of hand—in other words, with the ribald tolerance Voltaire would have brought to the circumstance—but as a degenerate, and a dangerously infectious one at that. Doctors are, of course, supposed to be free of such proscriptive attitudes, but there are always some who are as easily bent as anyone else by religion or ideology. Klotz was one of these, and while I'm sure that he was only doing his duty in tracking my history, his temper was chillingly adversarial. Also, he was, in my case, guilty of an act of omission that unalterably stamped him as a doctor who hated not the disease but its victims.

AS THE WINTRY DAYS and nights in the hospital wore on, and the Kahn tests continued to show my blood serum swarming with spirochetes, and I worried myself into a deeper and deeper feeling of hopelessness, I brooded over my past sex life, which seemed to me a paltry one, at least numerically speaking. By what improbable mischance had I sealed my doom? Even in those repressed years of the Bible Belt South, to have had at nineteen only three partners, two of whom I'd met in boozy mayfly matings already dimming in memory, scarcely made me feel like a red-hot lover, much less the randy alley cat generally associated with the disease. Still, as Winkler pointed out, even though syphilis was not as widespread as the clap, all it took was one quick poke in the wrong partner's hole and a man could be done for. Whose hole, then, and when? The actual encounters were all so recent, and together so few, that I could easily let my mind pounce on each one, trying to figure out which specific grappling had permitted the *T. pallidum* to begin its infestation.

On a bright morning, as I sat on my camp stool plunged into one of these self-lacerating reveries, Winkler came up with a mournful look to say that he was sorry but my Kahn remained "highly reactive." Then he announced that Dr. Klotz—finally, after many days—wished to see me, to take my case history. Was I religious? Winkler asked. When I said that I wasn't but asked him why he wanted to know, the corpsman rolled his eyes, then declared, "He's got a kind of narrow-minded view of things." He added, as he had once before, that it was all part of a "personal fixation."

As I look back on that time, I can see that Klotz, whatever the complexities of his motivation, had a need to squeeze the most out of the vindictive rage against syphilis already prevailing in the armed forces—one that mirrored the broader abhorrence in American society. While Klotz was doubtless not typical of navy doctors, or the medical profession in general, he was working well within the pious and cold-blooded restraints regarding sexually transmitted diseases that had prevailed in the navy for many years. During the First World War, President

Wilson's secretary of the navy, Josephus Daniels, a godly North Carolinian if there ever was one, made history in a small way by banishing alcohol from officers' wardrooms and elsewhere on naval ships and bases, thereby bringing to an end an ancient and cherished custom. But at least this created no mortal danger. In his intolerance of carnality, Daniels ruled against a proposal that sailors and marines be given free access to condoms, and thus became responsible for unnumbered venereally related illnesses and deaths. Apart from his own belief, Klotz was obviously the inheritor of a tradition with a firm root in southern Christian fundamentalism.

In presenting my case history to Klotz that morning, I had to describe my relations with a girl and two older women. Klotz referred to these as "exposures." While the doctor took notes, I told him that, almost exactly two years before, I had lost my virginity for two dollars in a walk-up hotel room in Charlotte, North Carolina. I was a college freshman, and the woman was about thirty-five. In answer to his question about whether I had used protection, I replied that I thought so but could not be sure, since I had drunk too much beer for clear memory. I then went on to the next exposure. (What I did not describe to Klotz was the interminable anxiousness of waiting in the dismal little hotel lobby while my anesthetized classmate, a raunchy dude from Mississippi, who had initiated our debauch, preceded me for what seemed hours with Verna Mae, which was what she called herself. Nor did I tell the doctor that my memory of Verna Mae was of an immensely sad and washed-out towhead in a stained slip and dirty pink slippers who raised a skinny arm and took my two dollars with such lassitude that I thought she might be ill; nor did I recount being nearly ill myself, from apprehension and a stomach-churning disbelief at the idea that what I'd awaited with anxious joy since the age of twelve was about to happen, something so unbearably momentous that I barely registered the words when, sliding the two bucks into her brassiere, she said in a countrified voice, "I sure hope you don't have to take as long as that friend of yours.")

The second exposure was a girl, age eighteen, a college sophomore I'll call Lisa Friedlaender. (It is a reflection on the aridity of sexual life in the forties—even, or, I should say, especially, on college campuses—that there was a gap of nearly a year and a half between Verna Mae and Lisa.) I told Klotz that I had met Lisa, who was from Kew Gardens, New York, at a college in Danville, Virginia, the previous spring. I was by then enrolled in the Marine V-12 program at Duke and had traveled up to Danville for a weekend. That weekend, we had had intercourse (a word that made me writhe but that Klotz encouraged), and we had had it many times after that, both protected and unprotected, on my weekend leaves in

April and May. She went home to Kew Gardens for summer vacation, and when she returned to Danville we resumed intercourse, having weekend sex until I was sent here, to Parris Island. I was certain that Lisa was not the source of the disease, I went on, since I was only her second partner and she was from a proper middle-class Jewish background, where the acquiring of such an illness was unlikely. (I had often wondered how a proper middle-class southern lad like me had come to deserve anyone as angelic as my ripe and lively Lisa, with her incontinent desires, which matched mine and were the real reason, though I didn't tell Klotz, for our frequent lack of protection: we were fucking so continuously and furiously that I ran out of condoms. My native Wasp folklore, which tended to idealize asthenic, inaccessible blondes, had not prepared me for this dark and lusty creature; we began rolling around on a moonlit golf green within two hours of our first meeting. I didn't tell this to Klotz, either, though Klotz the moral inquisitor at one point tipped his hand by demanding, "Were you in love?" To this I had no reply, having a sense that such a question really implied a policy decision. What of course was impossible to make Klotz understand about love was that if you were not yet twenty, and were a marine eventually headed for the Pacific who shared with your brothers the conviction that you would never see twenty-one, or a girl, ever again, and if the delirium of joy you felt the first time Lisa Friedlaender's nipples sprang up beneath your fingertips was love, then you were probably in love.)

My last exposure was a woman named Jeanette. Age about forty. I told Klotz that I was with a fellow marine in Durham when we picked up old Jeanette and a female friend at a barbecue joint one night during the past August. They were both employees of the Liggett & Myers factory, where they worked on an assembly line making cigarettes. I had intercourse with Jeanette only once, unprotected. (The subtext in the case was largely anaphrodisiac amnesia. As with Verna Mae, the beer I had consumed made memory a slide show of incoherent instants: a wobbling ramble through the dark, collapsing together on the cold ground of a Baptist churchyard, hard by a tombstone, and inhaling the sweet raw smell of tobacco in the frizzy hair of Jeanette, who had just come off the night shift. I remembered nothing of the act itself, but for some obscure reason, as my confession spilled forth, the recollection of the carton of Chesterfields she had given me left a taste of sadness.)

When I finished, Klotz fiddled with his notes for a moment, then said, "You betrayed the girl, didn't you?"

I nodded my miserable agreement but made no reply.

"Has it occurred to you that you might have infected her?"

Again I nodded, for the possibility of having passed on the contagion had lingered in my mind for days, jabbing me with fierce self-reproach.

"You probably were infected by the prostitute in Charlotte or the woman in Durham," the doctor said. "Syphilis is prevalent among lower-class southern white women. That's why it's dangerous to go roaming around in the wrong places if you can't practice abstinence."

I couldn't respond to this. Although I was smothered with regret, I felt no remorse and was not about to say that I was sorry.

"There's no way now of knowing which woman infected you. Suppose you just write a letter to that girl and tell her that she may have been exposed to syphilis. You should also tell her to get tested right away and have appropriate treatment."

I recall trying to retrieve, at that moment, some serene boyhood memory, a foolish escapade, any innocent event that might let me float above this anguish, but Klotz was too quick to permit me the solace.

"Nature has a way of compensating for nearly every reckless thing we do," he said.

A DAY OR TWO AFTER my interview with Klotz, the hospital corpsmen began to place tacky Christmas ornaments up around the ward; they painted a silver NOEL on the glass of the door and hung a hideous plastic trumpet-tooting angel from the central light fixture. The same day, I noticed that my gums were beginning to bleed. There had been some irritation before, but I had ignored the tenderness. This was serious bleeding. It was not "pink toothbrush," a symptom employed to help advertise Ipana, the hot toothpaste of the day. It was a slight but constant seepage of blood into my mouth, one that made me aware of the sweetish taste throughout the day and left a red stain on my handkerchief whenever I blotted it away. I could tell it was aggravated by smoking—but I kept steadily puffing. My gums had become raw and spongy, and that night the act of toothbrushing created a crimson cataract. I developed a feverish, cruddy feeling. I was terrified, but I kept my alarm to myself. The spirochetes were on the attack. There were countless ways the disease could make itself known, and I calculated that this was just one of them. When I told Winkler about my new trouble, he seemed puzzled, but said I should pay a visit to the hospital dentist, who might at least be able to relieve some of my distress. The dental officer was a dour man, trapped in routine, who offered neither comfort nor explanation; he did, however, swab out my mouth with a florid and repulsive lotion called gentian violet, a vial of which he gave me for daily application. It was an absurdity, a flimsy barrier against the onrushing ruin.

Days passed in a kind of suspended monotony of fear. Meanwhile, the weight of hopelessness, bearing down on my shoulders with almost tactile gravity I thought of a yoke in the animal, burdened-down sense—had become a daily presence; I felt a suffocating discomfort in my brain. Sitting on a camp stool next to my bed, remote from the other marines, I began to withdraw into the cocoon of my-self. The sex-demented clap patients, jabbering about cunt and pussy, magnified my despair. I lost my appetite. Out-side my window, marines marched in the distance on the asphalt drill field, exhaling clouds of frigid breath. The glittering white inlet of the ocean rolled endlessly east-ward like Arctic tundra. At night, after lights-out, I began to prowl the ward, padding about in anxiety until, return-ing to the stool, I would sit and stare at the expanse of water, dim in the starlight, and seemingly frozen solid. What a blessed relief it would be, I thought, to lie down and be encased in that overcoat of ice, motionless, without sensation and, finally, without care, gazing up at the indif-ferent stars.

I had kept up a busy correspondence during my early Marine Corps days. Fat envelopes, lots of them with ad-dresses in familiar handwriting, envelopes of various colors and lengths (some with a not-yet-stale hint of perfume), were gifts that guys in the service awaited with greedy suspense, like children at Christmastime. I kept my seabag stuffed with reread letters, and Lisa Friedlaender had written to me often at Parris Island. In that buttoned-up age, it was probably not all that common for letter-writing lovers to express their craziness in steamy strophes, but Lisa had a gifted hand. Her remembrances to me were generally graphic and sometimes astonishing; she was way ahead of her time. But those were letters I could not read any longer; the very packet, which I kept tied up with string, was cursed with a vile pathology. Nor, despite Klotz's order, could I bring myself to write to Lisa.

Instead, I addressed myself to another problem: that of maintaining my composure in the face of a final, insupportable outrage. One morning, Winkler brought me two letters—one from Lisa (I put it away, unread) and one from my stepmother. Only two years before, my father had married, for reasons I was never able to fathom, an ungainly, humorless, pleasure-shunning middle-aged spinster, and the antipathy we felt for each other had been almost as immediate as our differences were irreconcilable. She was an observant Christian, curiously illiberal for an Episcopalian, while I had proudly begun to announce my skepticism and my fealty to Camus, whose *Le Mythe de Sisyphe* I'd read laboriously but with happiness in French at Duke, and whose principles, when I outlined them to her, she deemed "diabolical." I thought her a prig; she considered me a libertine. She was a teetotaler; I drank—a lot. Once, frankly baiting her while a little crocked, I praised masturbation as a universal delight, and she denounced me to my father as a "pervert." (I *had* gone too far.) She was educated, intelligent, and that made her bigotry the more maddening. I preserved a chill truce with the woman because of my love for my misguided father. She was a teacher of nursing, actually quite a good one— even, in a way, distinguished (onetime district president of the Graduate Nurses Association)—and therein lay another contradiction: nurses, like doctors, were supposed to be free of the moralism that drove her to write a pious letter meant to make me writhe on the rack of my dereliction.

How appalled she and my father were, she wrote, at the terrible news. (I had sent them a letter in which I was disingenuous enough to say that I had been sidelined with "a little blood problem," an evasion she immediately scented.) The only serious blood problem I could have was one of the malignant diseases like leukemia, and I plainly didn't have that, given my remarks about feeling in such good health. She went on to predict, in her chilly, professional way, that in all likelihood I could be cured by the new antibiotics, *provided* the disease had not progressed too far into the CNS (central nervous system, she explained help-

fully, adding that the damage could be fearful and irreversible). Shifting into the spiritual mode, she informed
me that one could only pray that the illness had not yet
been invasive. She had no intention of judging me, she announced (pointing out that there was, of course, a Higher
Judge), but then she asked me to look back on my recent
way of life and ponder whether my self-indulgent behavior had not led to this—the words remain ineffaceable to
this day—"awful moment of truth." Finally, she hoped I
would be reassured that, in spite of her disapproval of the
conduct that had brought me to this condition, she cared
for me very, very much.

IN PONDERING THESE EVENTS of fifty years ago, I've
never felt seriously betrayed by memory—most of the
moments I've re-created are so fresh in my mind that they
have the quality of instant replay—but I know that I've
been slightly tricked from time to time, and I've had to ad-
just my account of these events. That memory could be a
clever deceiver was neatly demonstrated, when I began
finishing this chronicle, by my "Medical History"—a little
manual, faintly mildewed, with pages the color of a faded
jonquil—which surfaced among my Marine Corps me-
mentos while I was searching for something else. This is
the standard medical record that accompanies every ma-

rine throughout his career. While my lapses were minor, the "Medical History" showed me to be quite off the mark about certain matters of chronology. I could have sworn, for example, that I was still in the hospital until a few days before Christmas, when in fact I had been returned to duty by then; the awful Yuletide decorations I recalled must have adorned not the ward but my barracks, considerably later. Also, I have written of those apparently unceasing Kahn tests, a ritual that kept me tense with fear. It seems impossible to me now that I was not bled daily—as I awaited the results, I recall, I was nearly devoured by anxiety—but the "Medical History" shows that there were only five of these procedures in the course of a month. I'm fascinated by the fact that my tendentious memory lured me into exaggerating the number of times I experienced this torture.

But Dr. Klotz and his behavior have remained mysterious. The "Medical History" reveals only his routine notations and a final, meticulously clear signature. I think Klotz has compelled my attention (slightly this side of obsession) all these years because, to put it simply, he was frightening. He represented, in his bloodless and remote way, the authority figure that most people dread encountering but so often do meet face to face: the dehumanized doctor. In later years, I would come to know many exemplary physicians, but also more than one for whom my memory of Klotz provided a creepy prototype. I never fathomed Klotz's need to chasten those whom he conceived to be sexual hoodlums among all the miserable, unwell marines who showed up for his help. I wasn't alone among these miscreants. Was it religion (as Winkler had hinted) that gave him his hang-up, some narrow faith that had provided him with a view of sex that was as fastidious as it was harsh? Perhaps, as Winkler also suggested without contradiction, it wasn't religion so much as that "personal fixation." If that was true, it was a fixation animated by cruelty. Nothing else would account for his failure to tell me from the outset that there was a possibility that I didn't have syphilis at all.

Several days after I received the letter from my step mother, I was summoned to the end of the ward by Winkler, who led me into the tiny office of Klotz's second-in-command. Everyone called him Chief. He was a chief pharmacist's mate named Moss, a sandy-haired, overweight Georgian with a smoker's hack, good-heartedness written all over him. As in the past, he put me quickly at ease. He was an old man by my standards, probably thirty-five or older. I had come to trust and respect most of the medical corpsmen, like Moss and Winkler, who held out to sick marines a kind of spontaneous sympathy beyond the capacity of the doctors, or at least of the doctors I knew. And the feeling I had for Moss was not so tepid as mere respect; it was more like awe, for the year before he had taken part in the bloody landing at Tarawa, that slaughter-house beyond compare, and there he had risked his big ass to save the lives of more than one marine, winning a com-mendation in the process. Marines and sailors were tradi-tionally hostile to each other, but one could only regard someone like Moss with admiration, or even love, as I think I did that day. A couple of times before, he'd come by my sack to chat, always cheery and plainly eager to calm my fear, a good ol' boy from Valdosta, a bearlike, rather untidy guy who plainly conceived medicine to be a tender enterprise not entirely bound by technology. He told me that Lieutenant Commander Klotz had departed on Christmas leave but had left him instructions about my case. My case, in fact, was contained in a file on Moss's desk, and he said he wanted to talk to me about it.

First off, I didn't have syphilis.

I recall thinking, despite my apostasy, of Revelation: "He that overcometh shall inherit all things . . ."

"I had a talk on the phone with the chief dental officer," Moss said. "He told me what he told Dr. Klotz. Your Vin-cent's disease cleared up almost immediately. Just a couple of old-fashioned applications of gentian violet. Smile for me, boy."

I smiled widely, a big, shit-eating grin, and Moss heaved with laughter. "Damned if you don't look like a

Ubangi. Gentian violet. That old standby. The man who could find a way to get the violet out of gentian violet would make him some money."

"Tell me something, Chief," I said as Moss motioned for me to sit down. "If I get the situation correctly, my Kahn test has gone to negative. Zero. If this is true, and I guess it is, what's the connection?"

"Let me ask you a question," said Moss. "Did you ever have this condition—it's also called trench mouth—anytime before?"

I reflected for an instant, then said, "Yes, I believe I did, come to think about it. Up at Duke. There were these marines for a while—I was one of them—complaining about this inflammation in the mouth, and bleeding. I had it badly for some time, then it seemed to go away. I didn't think about it anymore. There was talk about it being spread by the unclean water we used to wash our trays in the mess hall. So tell me, Chief, what's the connection?"

Moss patiently explained to me what appeared to be the reason for Klotz's misdiagnosis, and what in fact had been behind the entire fiasco. He said that Klotz, after receiving the dental report, had written in my record book, "Dentist discharged patient for his Vincent's." That morning, Moss, out of curiosity, had followed up on this notation, checking out various venereal-disease manuals and textbooks for further enlightenment, and had discovered that the principal causes for false serological positives in the Kahn test were leprosy and yaws. (Jesus, I thought, leprosy and yaws!) There was no chance of my having acquired either of those exotic, largely hot-climate diseases, Moss went on. Klotz must have ruled them out all along, convinced (or, I thought, wanting to be convinced) that I had syphilis in a more or less advanced form. Moss said that Vincent's disease was mentioned as a possible cause, but a rare one—so rare that Klotz must have discounted it. I learned from Moss that despite Vincent's preposterously gruesome official name—acute necrotizing ulcerative gingivitis—the inflammation of the mouth itself was relatively mild and easy to treat, often with a single application to the gums of the powerful bactericide gentian violet. One of the causative organisms in Vincent's was another busy little spirochete (Moss spelled it out: *Treponema vincentii*), and it had shown up in my blood tests. With me there had been a recurrence of symptoms. "It's a good thing you finally went to the dentist," Moss concluded, "or you might have been here forever."

As much as I felt a friend and ally in the Chief, I still hesitated to state my case against Klotz, upon whom my rage and loathing grew more grimly focused, if that was possible, at every item Moss disclosed. I didn't want to strain the rapport I had with Moss by attacking his superior—for all I knew, though only God would know why, he might hold

Klotz in high esteem. At the same time, the evil suspicions that sprang to mind as Moss murmured his litany of details had actually begun to make me a little nauseated, taking the glow off my euphoria, and there was no way I could let the suspicions rest. I said, "You know, Chief, he wanted to find the worst things. I guess I was too intimidated to tell him I've had that little scar on my dick all my life." Then I said, "Anyway, what this means is that Dr. Klotz could have told me there was a possibility of a false positive. A possibility." I paused. "But he didn't do that."

"That's really right." Moss didn't wait an extra beat, uttering the words with a soft, rising inflection that had a distinct edge of contempt and carried its own conviction of wrongdoing. I knew then that he was on my side.

"He's read what you've read," I persisted. "He knew about Vincent's disease. He could have run me through that drill, couldn't he? But he didn't do that, either. He could have spared me a lot of misery. He could have given me some hope—"

"That's really right."

"What is this jerk's problem, Chief?"

Klotz was on leave. Within a few hours I would return to the barracks and the drill field, just another healthy recruit thrust back into the maw of the war machine. I would never see the Chief again. Under the circumstances, it would be safe for Moss to give voice to whatever innermost feelings he had toward Klotz. But Moss was too much the wise old salt, too professional, and, doubtless, too loyal to an honorable code to go that far. Still, I sensed a comradely affinity, and it was denunciation enough, a spiritual handclasp, when he squinted at me and said, "He was punishin' you, boy, punishin' you."

As I left the hospital that day, I looked forward to the ordeal that my phantom illness had interrupted. Mean corporals with taut shiny scalps and bulging eyes would be at me again, poking their swagger sticks into my solar plexus, ramming their knees up my butt, calling me a cocksucker and a motherfucking sack of shit, terrorizing me with threats and drenching me with spittle and hatred, making my quotidian world such a miasma of fright that each night I would crawl into my bed like an invalid seeking death, praying for resurrection in another life. After that, there was the bloody Pacific, where I would murder and perhaps be murdered. But those were horrors I could deal with; in that gray ward I'd nearly been broken by fears that were beyond imagining.

Late that afternoon, I trudged past the drill field in the waning light, packing my seabag on my shoulder, hefting a load that seemed pounds lighter than it had a month before. At the far end of the field, a platoon of marines was tramping across the asphalt, counting in cadence, a chorus of young voices over which one voice, the drill instructor's, soared in a high maniacal wail. In some undiscoverable distance, faint yet clear, a band played the "Colonel Bogey March," that jauntily sad evocation of warfare, its brassy harmonies mingling triumph and grief. The music made me walk along with a brisk step, and I felt it hurrying me toward a future where though suffering was a certainty, it wore a recognizable face.

I had just enough time for a stop at the PX, to stock up on cigarettes and candy bars. The candy was a clandestine indulgence I felt I owed myself, and couldn't resist. Nor could I resist, along with the Baby Ruths, buying a postcard showing a photograph of marines grinning insincerely as they performed calisthenics, and the caption "Greetings from Parris Island." Toward Christmas I addressed it to my stepmother, and scribbled:

Dear Old Girl,

My frantic, obsessive copulations produced not syphilis but trench mouth. (Escaped from the Clap Shack in time to celebrate the birth of our Lord and Savior.)

Much love, Bill

—*The New Yorker,* 18 SEPTEMBER 1995

"I'LL HAVE TO
ASK INDIANAPOLIS—"

THERE WAS A TIME IN MY LIFE WHEN INDIANAPO-
lis figured very large as an influence on me. About two
hundred years ago—it was 1951, to be exact—I finished
my first novel, *Lie Down in Darkness*. In those post–World
War II years there was a reverent, I should say almost *wor-
shipful,* aura that surrounded the writing and publishing of
novels. This is not to say that even today the novel as a literary form has lost cachet or distinction (though there are
critics who would argue that position), but in those days to
be a young novelist was a little like being a rock star in our
time. The grand figures of the previous generation—
Faulkner, Hemingway, Dos Passos, Sinclair Lewis, James
T. Farrell—were still very much alive, and we young
hopefuls were determined to emulate these heroes and
stake our claim to literary glory. The first among the new-
comers to make his mark was Truman Capote, whose brilliant tales and lovely novel *Other Voices, Other Rooms* filled

me, his exact contemporary, with inordinate envy. Soon after this came *The Naked and the Dead* by Norman Mailer, a writer of such obvious and prodigious gifts that it took the breath away. Following on Mailer's triumph was James Jones's monumental *From Here to Eternity,* which was quickly succeeded by that classic which forever crystallized the soul of the American adolescent, *The Catcher in the Rye* by J. D. Salinger. I don't think it was vainglory on my part, as I was writing my own novel and was watching these fine books appear one after another, to consider myself an authentic member of the same generation and to want to make *Lie Down in Darkness* a worthy companion to those works.

I wrote the first pages of *Lie Down in Darkness* while I was living in New York City in the basement of a brownstone on upper Lexington Avenue. It was the winter of 1947. I was twenty-three years old and had just been fired from my job as junior editor with the McGraw-Hill Book Company—a fiasco I described much later in another book of mine, *Sophie's Choice.* There was a blizzard raging outside—it's still memorialized in weather annals as the greatest New York blizzard of the century—and those opening pages were written in passion and in the incomparable assurance of youth, and were never later touched or revised.

After the blizzard subsided I had a stack of manuscript

pages and a burning desire to see them amplified with a full-fledged novel. But I sensed that I needed guidance and, even more than guidance, encouragement. I had heard of a lively and interesting class in fiction writing at the New School for Social Research, and I enrolled in this class, conducted by an engaging, scholarly teacher named Hiram Haydn. He was the ideal preceptor for a writing course, strict and no-nonsense regarding the substance of one's text, quick to detect softness or sloppiness or sentimentality, yet eager to find and nurture those radiant beams of true talent that occasionally appear in such a class. I was enormously pleased when I realized that he liked my work and, beyond that, thrilled that through him I was able to establish a publishing connection. For, as it turned out, Haydn had just been hired as New York editor of the Indianapolis-based house of Bobbs-Merrill. It also turned out that he had been given the authority to sign up for book contracts those among his students who he felt had literary promise. I sensed in Hiram an enormous zeal and idealism, a man determined to transform Bobbs-Merrill from a rather commercial enterprise, one whose chief previous glory had been the perennially huge best-seller *The Joy of Cooking*, into a publishing house that would honor and nurture good writing. And so I was flabbergasted and filled with joy when he offered me an option on my first novel and a check for an amount that was somewhat modest in those days, even by Indiana standards—one hundred dollars.

For the next three years I struggled to complete the book, moving all over the map, to North Carolina, to Brooklyn, to a small town up the Hudson River, to a cramped apartment that I shared with a young sculptor who was as poor as I was, on the Upper West Side of Manhattan. Money was a major problem for me—I had next to none except for a tiny stipend from my generous father—and the income I could expect derived entirely from what Hiram could shake from the coffers of Bobbs-Merrill. This is where the word *Indianapolis* began to loom large in my destiny. Whenever, literally down to my last single dollar, resorting to pawning the Elgin wristwatch I had received on my fifteenth birthday, or going to a grocery store and trying to redeem, for a box of frozen Birds Eye peas, the coupon my sculptor friend had received upon complaining about a worm he had found in another box of peas—when, in these straits, I approached Haydn for an advance on my royalties, the reply would come, "I'll have to ask Indianapolis." Mercifully, the response from this city was almost always favorable, ensuring my humble survival, but in any case the name *Indianapolis* acquired the quality of an incantation, rather portentous and ominous at the same time, like *Hanoi* during the time of Vietnam or *Moscow* throughout the Cold War.

The talismanic nature of Indianapolis became even more apparent somewhat later when, exhaustedly, I finished the last chapter of the book and went off as a marine lieutenant to Camp Lejeune, North Carolina, where I began training for combat in the Korean War. This was a dark time indeed. Firmly believing that in September, when the book was scheduled to be published, I would be fighting the Chinese in Korea, I spent the spring and summer despairingly in the Carolina swamps, at least part of the time correcting the galleys of *Lie Down in Darkness*. Where Indianapolis came in once again was through the views of Bobbs-Merrill's management over matters of literary taste and propriety.

That time—the late 1940s and early '50s—was a watershed period in our literature. Although some years earlier *Ulysses* had been approved by the federal courts for adult consumption, Joyce's masterpiece was virtually unique in being exempt from the scrutiny of the censors and the puritans. But in the years following World War II there began a profound if gradual change toward permitting writers to express themselves more freely, particularly in the use of the vulgar vernacular and in matters of sex. I emphasize the gradualness of the transition. For example, in *The Naked and the Dead*, published in 1948, Norman Mailer was forced to use, for the common vulgarism describing sexual intercourse, not the four-letter word but a

foreshortened three-letter epithet, *fug*. Among other results, this prompted the raunchy old actress Tallulah
Bankhead, upon meeting young Mailer for the first time,
to say, "Oh, you're the writer who doesn't know how to
spell *fuck*." But the times *were* changing. The first book in
American literature to employ this and other Anglo-Saxon
expletives with absolute freedom was James Jones's *From
Here to Eternity*; and even *The Catcher in the Rye*, published in that same year, 1951, used the word, although in a
way that was intended to demonstrate its offensiveness.
It's interesting, by the way, that even today *The Catcher in
the Rye* is among the books most frequently yanked off the
library shelves of public schools, usually at the behest of
angry parents who, ironically and certainly stupidly, seem
to be unaware that in this one case the word is seen by the
young hero, Holden Caulfield, as objectionable.

But what about *Lie Down in Darkness*, also published in
that turning-point year of 1951? As it developed, while I
was with the marines in North Carolina, Hiram Haydn
was having trouble with Indianapolis. The powers that
be at Bobbs-Merrill were getting upset over a few of the
situations and the dialogue in my about-to-be-published
manuscript. Unlike Mailer and Jones, I was writing of a
domestic fictional milieu in which the common four-letter
words were not employed frequently, at least at that time,
but I had retained a few of the more or less milder dirty

(Exclusively for Correspondence between Offices)

THE BOBBS-MERRILL COMPANY · INC.

Publishers

Memorandum for   Mr. Hiram Haydn   Date 4 23 51

Subject   Lie Down in Darkness

    This report from Mr. Ziegner (who has been reading
the manuscript without interrupting the proofroom) makes
some recommendations on literary grounds which invite
your friendly consideration.

    To me the report indicates that we are presented
with a publishing problem other than how many copies we
can sell—a problem of possible legal involvements.
Mr. Ziegner wishes to make it clear that with this
aspect he doesn't feel at all competent to express himself.

    Nor am I competent to reckon what the possible in-
volvements might be. I have kept only vague track of
the judicial decisions in so-called "obscenity" cases,
noting their increasing liberality. Whether Lie Down
in Darkness would fall within the precedents that have
been established, I do not know. Besides, ignoring
precedents is a favorite trick of present procedure,
every judge liking to write new law according to his
personal view.

    At any rate should we not approach this legal
problem objectively and seek the best informed opinion,
not only for the House's sake but for the author's?
What would you think, then, of consulting Melville
Cane? He is himself a literary artist and not narrow-
minded. He has dealt with such problems for other
publishers.

    If you approve this suggestion and have not a
copy of the script with all corrections in New York,
wire us and we will hold up setting type and send you
for the purpose the copy we've been working on.

DLC_S

---

*Memo from David L. Chambers, president of Bobbs-Merrill,
to Hiram Haydn, Styron's editor, about the bowdlerization of*
Lie Down in Darkness *(1951).* FROM THE ORIGINAL IN THE BOBBS-MERRILL
PAPERS, LILLY LIBRARY, INDIANA UNIVERSITY.

words, as they were called then, and several erotic situations that by present-day standards would seem amusingly tame. Nonetheless, Hiram Haydn, representing the New York office, found himself in conflict with the higher-ups in the Midwest office, and down in the Carolina boondocks I was caught in the cross fire. I remember some of Hiram's messages, which in those days, particularly because of my frequent inaccessibility, reached me by telegram. Once again the name of the capital city of Indiana took on the quality of an incantation. "Indianapolis," the wire would read, "suggests page 221 drop the word *ass*. Would you consider *bottom*?" Or, "Indianapolis concerned phrase page 140 *felt her up* too suggestive. Would you think of alternative?" And once I got a message that read, "Indianapolis will accept *big boobs* but will you still revise bit about *the open fly*."

Fortunately, these strictures and reservations did no permanent damage to my text; nor did I feel that my work suffered any major violation. I mostly managed to knuckle under for Indianapolis without complaint. But what I've said does show you how, at midcentury, there still existed in certain quarters in America a point of view about free expression that was severely circumscribed, still profoundly in thrall to nineteenth-century standards and to a prudery that now seems so quaint as to be almost touching. It could be said, of course, that we have gone over the

edge; indeed, there have been some books published in recent years that I've found so scabrous and loathsome that
I've yearned, at least for a moment, for a return to Victorian decorum and restraint. Yet my yearning is almost always short-lived. People, after all, are not *forced* to read
garbage, which, even if it overwhelms us—or seems to at
times—is preferable to censorship.

And this brings me to a consideration of what my
chronicle of *Lie Down in Darkness* and its problems has
been leading up to—and that is, in fact, freedom of expression in our time, and the importance of libraries to our
culture, and the danger that exists to the written word,
whether those words be dirty or clean, simple or sublime.
For it goes without saying that the written word is in peril,
and its enemies are not just the yahoos and the censors but
those who dwell in the academic camp.

Let me relate what recently happened to me. If you
write long enough you will inevitably suffer the misfor-
tune of having your words subjected to scholarly scrutiny.
This is much worse than getting bad reviews. Not long
ago I received in the mail a two-hundred-page thesis from
a graduate student at a California university that bore the
following title—I quote verbatim: "*Sophie's Choice:* A
Jungian Perspective." Beneath this was the description
"Prepared for Karl Kracklauer, Ph.D., for Partial Fulfillment of the Requirement for the Course 'Therapeutic

Process.'" I will now quote from the first page of the intro-duction: "As Styron's Sophie is a complicated character, and because her relationships are multifaceted and equally complex, I focus primarily on a single event in Sophie's life in order to gain entry into her psyche. In analyzing So-phie I rely on Greek mythology, Greek artwork and Jung-ian psychology." The important line: "In this paper I analyze the character Sophie from the *movie* 'Sophie's Choice.'" There was a footnote to this statement that read: "Where the movie was vague I referred to the book, *Sophie's Choice*, for clarification."

This, it seems to me, is the ultimate anti-literary story. It follows logically that I should want to say a few words about the most pro-literary of institutions, the library. After all, we're gathered here in behalf of a library. I'd like to describe how in my early life the library evolved from a forbidding place, ruled by frightening Minotaurs and guardian demons, into a refuge, the center of my soul's rescue, the friendliest place on earth.

When I was fourteen John Steinbeck's epic novel *The Grapes of Wrath* was published, to mixed reviews. While it was generally praised as a literary achievement, there were dissenters who were profoundly offended by some of the coarsely realistic language. It should be noted that this lan-guage is totally innocuous by present-day standards, con-taining none of the wicked four-letter vocables that have *even* plopped onto the pages of the new *New Yorker*. Still, the book had created enormous protest in some quarters; like many works of the period it had been threatened by a ban in—where else?—Boston. My schoolmate Knocky Floyd had somehow briefly gotten hold of a copy of *The Grapes of Wrath*, and he told me that if I, too, could obtain the book I would find on page 232 the word *condom*. Or perhaps it was in the plural—*condoms*. It was a word that was nowhere, even in the dictionaries of those pre–World War II years, nor was another Steinbeckian sizzler, that is, *whore*; the idea of seeing these words in print made me nearly sick with desire, though in fairness to myself I also wanted to read the story of the suffering Joad family. The elderly Miss Evans, God rest her soul, was the librarian who presided over the public library in my hometown in Tidewater Virginia, and it was she whom I confronted when, on a lucky day, I managed at last to find on its shelf one of five or six already smudged and dog-eared copies of this incredibly popular book. As she finished stamping the back page she handed me the book with an intense scowl and asked me my age; when I replied fourteen, she gave a kind of squeal and began to snatch the volume away. "Unfit! Unfit!" Miss Evans cried. "Unfit for your age!" There was a tugging match that both embarrassed and horrified me—she kept repeating "Unfit!" like a malediction—and I finally let her grab the book back in triumph.

The next episode in my depraved quest for sensation took place a year later, when I was fifteen, in New York City. It was my first trip to the metropolis, a vacation at Christmastime from my Virginia prep school. I had a single goal. More than the Statue of Liberty, more than Times Square, my mind was set on one thing. On my second day I trudged through the snow past the icicle-clad lions of the New York Public Library and into the catalog room, where I thumbed through the cards in search of a volume that had been spoken of at school as one of the most erotically arousing works ever printed. I don't exaggerate when I recall my heart being in a near-critical seizure when I located the card and the name of the author, Richard von Krafft-Ebing (1840–1902), and the title, almost brutal in its terrifying promise, *Psychopathia Sexualis*. Every schoolboy of that time wanted to read this Germanic compendium of sexual horrors. With the scrawled Dewey decimal number and the title in hand I made my way to the circulation desk. Miss Evans would have approved of her much younger male counterpart: his face wore a look of lordly contempt. He was tall; in those days I was short. He looked down at me as, in my changing voice, I croaked out my request; he said scathingly, "This book is for specialists. Are you a specialist in the field?"

"What field?" I replied feebly.

"Abnormal psychology. Are you a specialist?"

His tone and manner had so smothered me with humiliation that I was speechless; after a silent beat or two he said: "This book is not for young boys seeking a thrill."

The effect was catastrophic, nearly fatal; I slunk out of the New York Public Library, resolved never to enter a library again.

These countless years later I've been able to regard those incidents in the way one regards so many experiences that seem tragic at the time they happen; they were both educating and valuable. Recently, when I've pondered the issue of censorship and pornography I've remembered these moments of awful rejection and have seen that they comprise an object lesson. Of course, my own youth was a factor in having been denied, and neither of those books were pornography. Still, there's a point to be made. It was not prurience, not lust that impelled me to seek out these works but a far simpler instinct: curiosity. In a puritanical society—and America is, par excellence, a puritanical society—it is the veil of forbiddenness, as much as what lies behind the veil, that provokes the desire for penetration, if I may use the word. Had Miss Evans permitted me to read the word *condom*, or had I been able to while away a winter afternoon immersed in Krafft-Ebing, whose juiciest passages, I later learned, were obscured in a smoke screen of Latin, I might have fulfilled at least some of my curiosity and then returned to normal adolescent concerns. As it was, I remained heavy-spirited and restless with need. The present-day foes of sexually explicit writing and other depictions of sex, whether art or pornography, and those who would censor such works don't understand this underlying psychological reality and thus undermine their own cause. There is, it is true, a group, probably not very large, of super-enthusiasts for whom pornography is an obsession and a necessity. Joyce Carol Oates has likened these people to religious votaries: one might morally disagree with them even as one scorns so much seemingly displaced heat, but their requirements should be democratically tolerated and finally even respected. At the same time, the nearly universal availability of erotica has allowed most other people to take it or leave it; many find it somehow fulfilling, and there is nothing wrong with that. I suspect that the great mass of people, their curiosity blessedly satisfied, have discovered in the aftermath an excruciating monotony and have signed off for good. The censors who would reestablish the tyranny of my youth should quit at this point, accepting the fact that it's the sordid absolutism of denial—not what is made accessible—that turns people into cranks and makes them violent and mad.

After I experienced rejection, acceptance, and total im-

mersion in reading, the United States Marine Corps introduced me to the glories of the library. During World War
II, at the age of seventeen, I joined the marines but was
deemed too young to be sent right away into the Pacific
combat. I was delivered for a time, instead, to the V-12
program at Duke University, which then, as now, possessed one of the great college libraries of America. I'm
sure it was at least partially the Zeitgeist that led me into a
virtual rampage through those library shelves. When one
has intimations of a too early demise it powerfully focuses
the mind. The war in the Pacific was at a boiling fury, and
there were few of us young marines who didn't have a pre-
vision of himself as being among the fallen martyrs. I was
taking a splendid course in seventeenth-century English
prose and I'd hoarded an incantatory line from Sir
Thomas Browne: *The long habit of living indisposeth us for
dying*. This, of course, is British understatement. I wanted
desperately to live, and the books in the Duke University
library were the rocks and boulders to which I clung
against my onrushing sense of doom and mortality. I read
everything I could lay my hands on. Even today I can recall the slightly blind and bloodshot perception I had of
the vaulted Gothic reading room, overheated, the smell of
glue and sweat and stale documents, winter coughs, whis-
pers, the clock ticking toward midnight as I raised my eyes
over the edge of *Crime and Punishment*. The library be-

came my hangout, my private club, my sanctuary, the place of my salvation; during the many months I was at Duke, I felt that when I was reading in the library I was sheltered from the world and from the evil winds of the future; no harm could come to me there. It was doubtless escape of sorts but it also brought me immeasurable enrichment. God bless libraries.

It's hard for me to realize that this was exactly fifty years ago, perhaps to this very night. Truly still, *the long habit of living indisposeth us for dying*. I forgot to mention that among the books at the Duke library I desperately wanted to read in those days, but was unable to obtain, were *Lady Chatterley's Lover* by D. H. Lawrence and *Tropic of Cancer* by Henry Miller. I did, however, see them incarcerated, immobilized like two child molesters, behind heavy wire grillwork in the Rare Book Room. I've learned that they were finally set free some years ago with an unconditional pardon.

—*Traces* (Indiana Historical Society), SPRING 1995

(originally delivered as an address
at the Indianapolis–Marion County
Public Library, 14 APRIL 1994)

LES AMIS DU PRÉSIDENT

In 1948, WHEN I HAD JUST BECOME OLD ENOUGH TO participate in an election, I cast my first vote for that durable old socialist presidential candidate Norman Thomas. This, of course, was a protest against both Harry Truman and Thomas E. Dewey—a throwaway vote—and I have always cast a Democratic ballot since then, although many times despairingly. And so, this past May, when I received a personal invitation to attend the inaugural of François Mitterrand as the president of France, my great surprise was accompanied by a fleeting wonder whether the honor was not perhaps acknowledgment of that lonely vote cast thirty-three years ago. But of course not: François Mitterrand, perhaps alone among chiefs of state of our time, cares for writers more than the members of any other profession—more than lawyers, more than scientists, more even than politicians—and his invitation to me and to six other writers was a simple confirmation of that concern. This nonpolemical account is that of a partisan.

It is interesting, I think, that among *les amis du président*—the small group of 125 or so of us who gathered at the Arc de Triomphe for the inaugural ceremony there were no representatives whatever of the diplomatic corps, no members of international officialdom, and a very minimum of pomp and circumstance. Interesting, too, that there were no French writers—obviously to avoid factionalism and jealousy. Two American writers stood with me, all of us dressed informally in ties and jackets: the playwright Arthur Miller and Elie Wiesel, novelist and essayist, chronicler of the Holocaust. The others, dressed similarly, were the Colombian novelist Gabriel García Márquez, the Mexican writer Carlos Fuentes, Julio Cortázar from Argentina, and Yachar Kemal of Turkey. Having gathered early, a little after noon under a gray sky threatening rain, we were able to observe the other guests as they arrived beneath the great arch with its engraved roll call of battles.

What these personages represented was unequivocal: the heart and marrow of world socialism. They came almost at random, without ceremony. Willy Brandt arrived, followed by Felipe González, head of Spain's Socialist Workers' Party. There was Olof Palme of Sweden. After him came socialist leaders Mário Soares of Portugal and

Bettino Craxi of Italy. Léopold Senghor, the president of Senegal and also a poet and writer, arrived, and shortly after came Andreas Papandreou, leader of the Socialist Party of Greece. But this was not an all-male gathering. Papandreou walked side by side with a radiant Melina Mercouri, whose post as member of the Greek Parliament now competes with her career as actress. Finally, in rather somber reminder of the tragic events of Chile and the eclipse of democracy there, Hortensia Allende appeared. The widow of the slain president was accompanied by another widow, the wife of Pablo Neruda, Chile's great poet. All in all, it was an extraordinary sight, this gathering of illuminaries and votaries of a cause which had been lost so often throughout European history that its unexpected triumph here had left everyone looking a little bit stunned and solemn. Plainly the mood was celebratory, but the shock of the win was too great and the people seemed to move unsteadily, a little as if at a funeral.

The arrival of Mitterrand was rather anticlimactic. The new president is the quintessential Frenchman: in his plain dark business suit he would merge into a Parisian crowd as indistinguishably as yet another rather well-fleshed lycée professor or lawyer or even the patron of a good restaurant. Thus he looked undeniably the common citizen when he bent down and placed flowers in front of the Eternal Flame, but the sound of "La Marseillaise" played by the army band raised in all of us, I could tell, the same old familiar chill.

At the luncheon at the Elysée Palace I found myself seated next to Claude Cheysson, who had not yet been named foreign minister but who, in an unpretentious way, gave the impression that he knew he was about to be tapped. He is an engaging and articulate man, and he asked me what I thought of the occasion, especially what my feelings were in regard to having been invited, along with the other writers. I said I was certain that all of the writers felt they were paying their respects to a man who, more than any other leader of a major Western nation, seemed prepared to insist on fuller measures on behalf of human rights, and that his presence on the world stage would be a significant corrective to the general rightward drift of power. In a lighter context, I added, writers were very rarely accorded this kind of recognition, especially in the United States—where, since John F. Kennedy at least, such honor was usually heaped upon rock stars, stand-up comedians, and golf champions—and that it was simply fun to help celebrate this day with a president who was so obviously and passionately in love with the written word. (Richard Eder, Paris correspondent of the *New York Times,* later alluded to our literary presence as part of the "froth" of nouveau radical chic surrounding Mitterrand, but he is wrong. A concern for culture and the intellect is not mere style with Mitterrand but central to his being.) As for Reagan, I told Cheysson, who seemed puzzled by our leader, it was not at all surprising that Americans would finally elect a movie actor as president. To the contrary, it was inevitable, since the American people have glorified movie stars to the point of lunacy and ever since the dawn of the cinema have yearned for a matinee idol to run the ship of state. Cheysson looked depressed but seemed to understand.

The socialist leveling process did not, at this luncheon, extend to the food, which began with *pâté de foie gras truffé des Landes* (a delectable dish originating in Mitterrand's native region), accompanied by a Château d'Yquem 1966, and ended, after an incredible raspberry dessert, with Dom Pérignon champagne 1971. *Time* magazine had reported that Mitterrand is indifferent to food, but here again the reporting was wrong. I was sitting only a few seats away from the president, and one could tell from the gusto with which he put away the elegant white spears of asparagus that he cares at least as much about eating as he does about attractive young women—all of these admirable tastes transcending party politics.

Afterward we stood in the garden of the palace and chatted with Mitterrand. For better or for ill, I was aware of no cordon of security guards, only Mitterrand himself looking a little withdrawn and ill at ease, but enjoying himself nonetheless as he talked with the well-wishers. There was a remarkable atmosphere of casualness. It might have been a garden party almost anywhere in France. The conversation, while not exactly momentous, sticks in the mind. When we spoke of America, Mitterrand seemed as mystified about the country as Cheysson had been about Reagan. "A vast, strange continent," he said, "so enormous and mysterious, so difficult to understand. But the people are wonderful. I wish I could say the same for your foreign policy."

When Elie Wiesel asked what it felt like to be president, Mitterrand paused, and a look of honest surprise came to his face. "I still can't believe it," he murmured. Such fine candor required from me the old Norman Thomas rooter—a compliment, and I told him that I had voted for him in my heart. He spoke in English for the first time. "I appreciate that," he said.

Toward the end of the afternoon we were scheduled to join with the other *amis du président* for a triumphal walk up the short street that leads at a right angle from the boulevard Saint-Michel to the Pantheon. Miller, Wiesel, Fuentes, and myself set off in our car, but the driver became confused and let us off not at a point where we could gain admission to the intersection but at a corner in the midst of the crowd. The throng in the streets was enthusiastic, noisy, wildly cheerful, and unbelievably huge. Both

Fuentes, who had been Mexican ambassador to France in the mid-1970s, and Wiesel, who had lived for a long time in Paris after World War II, said they had never seen such droves of people in the streets. Only the very cheerfulness of the mob prevented it from seeming menacing. People were everywhere—along the curbs, in the alleys, and on the sidewalks, waiting for the presidential motorcade to cruise up the boulevard to the intersection.

Meanwhile, the four North American writers were unable to penetrate the crowd or to get past the barricades that firmly lined the boulevard. Over and over again we tried to push through, waving our cards of admittance, but there was simply no way to penetrate the throng. In despair, we were about to give up and go to a bar and look at the proceedings on television when we spied Melina Mercouri in her car, accompanied by Andreas Papandreou, also hopelessly blocked. It was she who saved the entire situation. After a hurried conference with the four of us, she debarked from the car and pushed her way to the barricade. There, with pleading, with Greek gesticulations, and with overwhelming charm, she persuaded a very senior police official to let us through the barricade.

And now ensued the most remarkable procession any of us could remember. The broad boulevard Saint-Michel, utterly deserted but lined on either side by tens of thousands of people. Starting up its center four writers, the president of the Socialist Party of Greece, and Melina Mercouri, whose presence brought forth a vast roar from the crowd as she grinned gloriously and brandished a socialist rose. A heady and thrilling moment indeed, even when—as Fuentes pointed out—the crowd surely thought that the five gentlemen in their raincoats were Mercouri's bodyguards.

This is not the place to reflect on the future of socialism in France. That night at dinner some very rich Parisians I know dined on lobster as if at a wake, casting bleak auguries for the future, their voices heavy with bereavement. The history of the Socialist Party in Europe is hardly one of unalloyed success, and who knows what vicissitudes of the future might mock François Mitterrand's day of glory, as they might mock Ronald Reagan's or, for that matter, that of any man bold and brave enough to seek power. But as a fellow writer I found it very difficult—as we all stood in drizzling rain on the ancient gray steps of the Pantheon, listening to Beethoven's "Ode to Joy" while Mitterrand basked serenely in his hard-earned triumph—not to reciprocate the feeling of the inscription to me he wrote that day in one of his own books: "In gratitude and in hope."

—*The Boston Globe*, 26 JULY 1981

CELEBRATING CAPOTE

TRUMAN AND I WERE APPROXIMATELY THE SAME age, although when I got to know him he always insisted that I was six weeks older. This was not accurate—it turned out that *I* was several *months* younger than he was—but it doesn't matter. I make this point only to underline the appalling chagrin I felt, in my tenderest years as an aspiring, unpublished writer, when I read some of Truman's earliest work. The first story of his that I read was, I believe, published in *Mademoiselle*. After I finished it, I remember feeling stupefied by the talent in those pages. I thought myself a pretty good hand with words for a young fellow, but here was a writer whose gifts took my breath away. Here was an artist of my age who could make words dance and sing, change color mysteriously, perform feats of magic, provoke laughter, send a chill up the back, touch the heart—a full-fledged master of the language before he was old enough to vote.

I had read many splendid writers by that time, but in Truman I discovered a brand-new and unique presence, a storyteller whose distinctive selfhood was embedded in every sentence on the page. I was of course nearly sick with envy, and like all envious artists I turned to the critics for some corroboration of that mean little voice telling me that he wasn't all that good. *Ornamental* and *mannered* were the words I was looking for, and naturally I found them, for there are always critics driven wild by the manifestation of talent in its pure, energetic exuberance. But basically I knew better, as did the more discerning critics, who must have seen—as I saw, in my secret reckoning— that such gemlike tales as "Miriam" and "The Headless Hawk" had to rank among the best stories written in English. If they were ornamental or mannered, they corresponded to those adjectives in the same way that the finest tales of Henry James or Hawthorne or Edgar Allan Poe do, creating the same troubling resonance.

Needless to say, it is only the most gifted stylists who inspire imitation, and I confess to having imitated Truman in those days of my infancy as a writer. There is a wonderful story of his called "Shut a Final Door," which details the neurotic anguish of a young man living near Gramercy Park, that still captures the atmosphere of Manhattan during a summer heat wave better than almost any work I know. Not too long ago, I unearthed from among some old papers of mine a short story I wrote during that period, and it seems to be written in a manner almost plagiaristically emulative of Truman's story, containing nearly everything in "Shut a Final Door," including the heat wave and the neurotic young man— everything, that is, except Truman's remarkable sensibility and vision. When his first novel, *Other Voices, Other Rooms,* appeared and I read it, flabbergasted anew by this wizard's fresh display of his narrative powers, his faultless ear—the luxuriant but supple prose, everywhere under control—my discomfort was monumental. If you will forgive the somewhat topical reference, let me say that, although my admiration was nearly unbounded, the sense I felt of being inadequate would have made the torment of Antonio Salieri appear to be dull and resigned equanimity.

A few years later, my own first novel, *Lie Down in Darkness,* was published. Among the early reviews I read was one by Lewis Gannett in the *Herald Tribune*—a mildly favorable appreciation that noted my indebtedness to the following: William Faulkner, F. Scott Fitzgerald, and Truman Capote. I was a little crestfallen. I thought I had become my own man, you see, but Truman's voice was a hard one to banish entirely.

Shortly after this, I met Truman for the first time, during a Roman soirée. I was left with three separate, distinct memories of the evening: he was accompanied by a mistrustful-looking black mynah bird, whom he called Lola and who perched gabbling on his shoulder; he told me that I should definitely marry the young lady I was with, which, as a matter of fact, I did; and he informed me with perfect aplomb that he had been written up in all twelve departments of *Time* magazine, with the exception of "Sport" and "Medicine." We became friends after that. Although we were not close, I always looked forward with pleasure to seeing him, and I think the feeling was reciprocal. I somehow managed to avoid those sharp fangs he sank into some of his fellow writers, and I took it as a professional compliment of a very high order when, on several occasions, something I had written that he liked elicited a warm letter of praise. Generally speaking, writers are somewhat less considerate of each other than that.

A certain amount of Truman's work might have been a little fey, some of it insubstantial, but the bulk of the journalism he wrote during the following decades was, at its best, of masterly distinction. His innovative achievement, *In Cold Blood,* not only was a landmark in terms of its concept but possesses both spaciousness and profundity—a rare mingling—and the terrible tale it tells could only be told by a writer who had dared to go in deep and brush flesh with the demons that torment the American soul. Shrewd, fiercely unsentimental, yet filled with a mighty compassion, it brought out all that was the best in Truman's talent: the grave, restrained lyricism, the uncanny insights into character, and that quality which has never been perceived as the animating force in most of his work—a tragic sense of life.

Truman's work is now solidly embedded in American literature. Certainly it is possible to mourn the fact that the latter part of his too early ended life seemed relatively unproductive, but even this judgment is presumptuous, since I doubt that few of us have ever had to wrestle with the terrors that hastened his end. Meanwhile, let us celebrate the excellence of the work he gave us. Like all of us writers, he had his deficiencies and he made his mistakes, but I believe it to be beyond question that he never wrote a line that was not wrested from a true writer's anguished quest for the best that he can bring forth. In this he was an artist—I think even at times a great one—from the top down to the toes of his diminutive, somehow heroic self.

—*Vanity Fair*, DECEMBER 1984

JIMMY IN THE HOUSE

JAMES BALDWIN WAS THE GRANDSON OF A SLAVE. I was the grandson of a slave owner. We were virtually the same age and both bemused by our close link to slavery, since most Americans of our vintage—if connected at all to the Old South—have had to trace that connection back several generations. But Jimmy had vivid images of slave times, passed down from his grandfather to his father, a Harlem preacher of fanatical bent who left a terrifying imprint on his son's life. Jimmy once told me that he often thought the degradation of his grandfather's life was the animating force behind his father's apocalyptic, often incoherent rage.

By contrast my impression of slavery was quaint and rather benign; in the late 1930s, at the bedside of my grandmother who was then close to ninety, I heard tales of the two little slave girls she had owned. Not much older than the girls themselves at the outset of the Civil War, she knitted stockings for them, tried to take care of them through the privations of the conflict, and, at the war's end, was as wrenched with sorrow as they were by the enforced leave-taking. When I told this classic story to Jimmy he didn't flinch. We both were writing about the tangled relations of blacks and whites in America, and because he was wise Jimmy understood the necessity of dealing with the preposterous paradoxes that had dwelled at the heart of the racial tragedy—the unrequited loves as well as the murderous furies. The dichotomy amounted to an obsession in much of his work; it was certainly a part of my own, and I think our common preoccupation helped make us good friends.

Jimmy moved into my studio in Connecticut in the late fall of 1960 and stayed there more or less continuously until the beginning of the following summer. A mutual friend had asked my wife and me to give Jimmy a place to stay, and since he was having financial problems it seemed a splendid idea. Baldwin was not very well known then—except perhaps in literary circles, where his first novel, *Go Tell It on the Mountain,* was gradually gaining momentum—and he divided his time between writing in the cottage and trips out to the nearby lecture circuit, where he made some money for himself and where, with his ferocious oratory, he began to scare his predominately well-to-do, well-meaning audiences out of their pants.

Without being in the slightest comforted as a southerner, or let off the hook, I understood through him that black people regarded *all* Americans as irredeemably raciot, the most sinful of them being not the Georgia redneck (who was in part the victim of his heritage) but any citizen whatever whose de jure equality was a façade for de facto enmity and injustice.

Jimmy was writing his novel *Another Country* and making notes for the essay *The Fire Next Time*. I was consolidating material, gathered over more than a decade, for a novel I was planning to write on the slave revolutionary Nat Turner. It was a frightfully cold winter, a good time for the southern writer, who had never known a black man on intimate terms, and the Harlem-born writer, who had known few southerners (black or white), to learn something about each other. I was by far the greater beneficiary. Struggling still to loosen myself from the prejudices and suspicions that a southern upbringing engenders, I still possessed a residual skepticism: could a Negro *really* own a mind as subtle, as richly informed, as broadly inquiring and embracing as that of a white man?

My God, what appalling arrogance and vanity! Night after night Jimmy and I talked, drinking whiskey through the hours until the chill dawn, and I understood that I was in the company of as marvelous an intelligence as I was ever likely to encounter. His voice, lilting and silky, became husky as he chain-smoked Marlboros. He was spellbinding, and he told me more about the frustrations and anguish of being a black man in America than I had known until then, or perhaps wanted to know. He told me exactly what it was like to be denied service, to be spat at, to be called "nigger" and "boy."

What he explained gained immediacy because it was all so new to me. This chronicle of an urban life, his own life, was unself-pityingly but with quiet rage spun out to me like a secret divulged, as if he were disgorging in private all the pent-up fury and gorgeous passion that a few years later, in *The Fire Next Time,* would shake the conscience of the nation as few literary documents have ever done. We may have had occasional disputes, but they were usually culinary rather than literary; a common conviction dominated our attitude toward the writing of fiction, and this was that in the creation of novels and stories the writer should be free to demolish the barrier of color, to cross the forbidden line and write from the point of view of someone with a different skin. Jimmy had made this leap already, and he had done it with considerable success. I was reluctant to try to enter the mind of a slave in my book on Nat Turner, but I felt the necessity and I told Jimmy this. I

James Baldwin

ginning—and neither can this be overstated—a Negro just cannot *believe* that white people are treating him as they do; he does not know what he has done to merit it. And when he realizes that the treatment accorded him has nothing to do with anything he has done, that the attempt of white people to destroy him—for that is what it is—is utterly gratuitous, it is not hard for him to think of white people as devils. For the horrors of the American Negro's life there has been almost no language. The privacy of his experience, which is only beginning to be recognized in language, and which is denied or ignored in official and popular speech—hence the Negro idiom—lends credibility to any system that pretends to clarify it. And, in fact, the truth about the black man, as a historical entity and as a human being, *has* been hidden from him, deliberately and cruelly; the power of the white world is threatened whenever a black man refuses to accept the white world's definitions. So every attempt is made to cut that black man down—not only was made yesterday but is made today. Who, then, is to say with authority where the root of so much anguish and evil lies? Why, then, is it not possible that all things began with the black man and that he was perfect—especially since this is precisely the claim that white people have put forward for them-

83

Styron's marginalia in his copy of James Baldwin's
The Fire Next Time *(1963).*

am certain that it was his encouragement—so strong that it was as if he were daring me not to—that caused me finally to impersonate a black man.

Sometimes friends would join us. The conversation would turn more abstract and political. I am surprised when I recall how certain of these people—well-intentioned, tolerant, "liberal," all the postures Jimmy so intuitively mistrusted—would listen patiently while Jimmy spoke, visibly fretting then growing indignant at some pronouncement of his, some scathing aperçu they considered too ludicrous for words, too extreme, and launch a polite counterattack. "You can't mean anything like that!" I can hear the words now. "You mean—*burn* . . ." And in the troubled silence, Jimmy's face would become a mask of imperturbable certitude. "Baby," he would say softly and glare back with vast glowering eyes, "yes, baby. I mean *burn*. We will *burn your cities down*."

Lest I give the impression that that winter was all grim, let me say that this was not so. Jimmy was a social animal of nearly manic gusto and there were some loud and festive times. When summer came and he departed for good, heading for his apotheosis—the flamboyant celebrity that the 1960s brought him—he left a silence that to this day somehow resonates through the house.

In 1967, when *The Confessions of Nat Turner* was pub-

lished, I began to learn with great discomfort the conse-
quences of my audacity in acquiring the persona of a black
man. With a few distinguished exceptions (the historian
John Hope Franklin for one), black intellectuals and writers expressed their outrage at both the historical imposture
I had created and my presumption. But Jimmy Baldwin remained steadfast to those convictions we had expressed to
each other during our nighttime sessions six years before.
In the turmoil of such a controversy I am sure that it was
impossible for him not to have experienced conflicting loy-
alties, but when one day I read a public statement he made
about the book—"He has begun the common history—
ours"—I felt great personal support but, more importantly, the reaffirmation of some essential integrity. After
those days in Connecticut I never saw him as often as I
would have liked, but our paths crossed many times and
we always fell on each other with an uncomplicated sense
of joyous reunion.

Much has been written about Baldwin's effect on the
consciousness of the world. Let me speak for myself. Even
if I had not valued much of his work—which was flawed,
like all writing, but which at its best had a burnished elo-
quence and devastating impact—I would have deemed his
friendship inestimable. At his peak he had the beautiful
fervor of Camus or Kafka. Like them he revealed to me the

core of his soul's savage distress and thus helped me shape and define my own work and its moral contours. This would be the most appropriate gift imaginable to the grandson of a slave owner from a slave's grandson.

—*The New York Times Book Review,*

20 DECEMBER 1987

TRANSCONTINENTAL WITH TEX

ONE OF MY ODDEST TRIPS IN A LIFETIME OF ODD
trips was the one I took with Terry Southern across the
U.S.A. in 1964. At that time I'd known Terry (whom I also
called, depending on mood and circumstance, "Tex" or
"T") ever since 1952 during a long sojourn in Paris. Like a
patient in lengthy convalescence, the city was still war
weary, with its beauty a little drab around the edges. Bicy-
cles and motorbikes clogged the streets. The *Paris Review*
was then in its period of gestation, and the principals involved in its development, including George Plimpton
and Peter Matthiessen, often spent their late evening hours
in a dingy nightspot called Le Chaplain, tucked away on
a back street in Montparnasse. In the sanatorium of our
present smoke-free society it is hard to conceive of the
smokiness of that place; the smoke was ice-blue, and almost like a semisolid. You could practically take your fin-
ger and carve your initials in it. It was smoke with a

searing, promiscuous smell, part Gauloises and Gitanes, part Lucky Strikes, part the rank bittersweet odor of pot. I was new to pot, and the first time I ever met Terry he offered me a roach.

I was quite squeamish. Marijuana was in its early dawn as a cultural and spiritual force, and the idea of inhaling some alarmed me. I connected the weed with evil and depravity. We were sitting at a table with Terry's friends, the late film director Aram ("Al") Avakian and a self-exiled ex–New York state trooper and aspiring poet whose name I've forgotten but who looked very much like Avakian, that is to say mustachioed and alternately fierce and dreamy-eyed. Also present was a *Paris Review* cofounder, the late Harold L. ("Doc") Humes, who had befriended me when I first arrived in Paris and was no stranger to pot. The joint Terry proffered disagreed with me, causing me immediate nausea; I recall Terry putting down this reaction to the large amount of straight brandy I'd been drinking, cognac being the *boisson de choix* in those days before Scotch became a Parisian commonplace. Terry responded quite humanely, I thought, to my absence of cool. He was tolerant when, on another occasion, I had the same queasy response. In our get-togethers, therefore, I continued to abuse my familiar substance, and Terry his, though he could also put away considerable booze.

I was living then in a room that Doc Humes had found

for me, at a hotel called the Libéria that had been his home for a year or so. The hotel was on the little rue de la Grande Chaumière, famous for its painters' ateliers; my Spartan room cost the equivalent of eight dollars a week, or eight dollars and a half if you paid extra to get the henna-dyed Gorgon who ran the place to change the sheets weekly. The room had a bidet, but you had to walk half a mile to the toilet. You could stroll from the hotel in less than two minutes to La Coupole or to the terrace of Le Dôme, Hemingway's old hangout, which also reeked of pot or hash and featured many young American men sitting at tables with manuscripts while affecting the leonine look of Hemingway, right down to the mustache and hirsute chest. I even overheard one of those guys address his girl companion as "Daughter." Terry and I would sit after lunch on the terrace, drinking coffee and smirking at these poseurs.

Terry was really hard up for money in those days, even in a Paris where a franc went a long way. I wasn't rich myself but I was, after all, a recently published bestselling author, and I could occasionally buy him a meal. We ate a couple of times in a cramped but excellent bistro on the avenue du Maine and had such luncheons as the following, which I recorded in a notebook: *entrecôte, pommes frites, haricots verts, carafe de vin, tarte tatin, café filtre.* Price for *two:* $3.60. The U.S. dollar was, of course, in a state of loony ascendancy, for which the French have been punishing us ever since; if, in addition, you exchanged your traveler's checks for the fat rate given by Maurice Loeb, the cheerful *cambiste* who hung out on the rue Vieille du Temple, in the Jewish Quarter, you could really become a high roller in 1952. It was one of the reasons the Communists plastered *U.S. Go Home* signs on every available wall.

That June I was busy in my room each afternoon, writing on a manuscript that would eventually become my short novel *The Long March*. One afternoon, unannounced, Terry showed up with his own manuscript and asked me if I would read it. His manner was awkward and apologetic. I knew he was working on a novel; during our sessions on the terrace of Le Dôme he had spoken of his serious literary ambitions. I had met a lot of Texans in the marines, most of whom lived up to their advance reputation for being yahoos and blowhards, and I never thought I'd encounter a Texan who was a novelist. Or a Texan who was really rather shy and unboastful. The manuscript he brought me made up the beginning chapters of *Flash and Filigree,* and I was amazed by the quality of the prose, which was intricately mannered though evocative and unfailingly alive. The writing plainly owed a debt to Terry's literary idol, the British novelist Henry Green, one of those sui generis writers you imitated upon pain of death, but nonetheless what I read of *Flash and Filigree* was fresh and exciting, and later

I told him so. Even then he had adopted that mock-pompous style that was to become his trademark, yet I sensed a need for real encouragement when he said: "I trust then, Bill, that you think this will put me in the quality lit game?" I said that I had no doubt that it would (and it did, when it was finally published), but as usual his talk turned to the need to make some money. "De luxe porn" was an avenue that seemed the most inviting—lots of Americans in Paris were cranking out their engorged prose—and of course it was one of the routes he eventually took, culminating a few years later in the delectable *Candy*. For Tex, success was on the way.

I didn't see a great deal more of Terry in Paris. That summer I went off to the south of France and, later, to live in Rome. But back in the States Terry was very much a part of the quality lit scene in New York during the next twenty years, frequenting places like George Plimpton's and, later, Elaine's, where I too hung out from time to time. He had great nighttime stamina, and we closed up many bars together. He bought a house in the remote village of East Canaan, not very far from my own place in Connecticut. And it was either at this house or mine that we decided to make a transcontinental trip together. I had been invited to give a talk at a California university, while Terry, having collaborated on the screenplay of Stanley Kubrick's *Dr. Strangelove*, a great hit, had been asked to come out to the coast to write the script for a film version of Evelyn Waugh's *The Loved One*. It was a perfect vehicle, I thought, to hone his gift for the merrily macabre. But the catalytic force for the whole trip was Nelson Algren. Nelson had written me, asking me to visit him in Chicago. The two of us had become friends and drinking companions during several of his trips to New York from Chicago, a city with which he had become identified as closely as had such other Windy City bards as Saul Bellow and Carl Sandburg and Studs Terkel. In his letter he said that he'd show me the best of Chicago. I had for some reason never been to Chicago, and so Terry suggested that we go west together and stop by and make a joint visit to Nelson, with whom he had also become pals. He had the notion of doing the Chicago–Los Angeles leg by train since soon, as he astutely predicted, no one would be traveling on the rails except the near destitute and those terrified by airplanes. By taking the fabled Super Chief of the Santa Fe, he pointed out, we'd be able to get a last glimpse of the great open spaces and also of the sumptuous club cars upon whose banquettes the movie bigwigs and sexy starlets had cavorted while the prairies whizzed by. It would be a precious slice of Americana soon to be foreclosed to travelers in a hurry, and I thought it was a fine idea.

Nelson was in his mid-fifties, one of the original hipsters. He had been telling stories about junkies and pimps

and whores and other outcasts while Kerouac and Fer-
linghetti were still adolescents, and had nailed down as his
private literary property the entire grim world of the
Chicago underclass. After years of writing, including a
stint with the W.P.A. Federal Writers' Project during the
Depression and another one hammering out venereal-
disease reports for the Chicago Board of Health, he hit it
big with *The Man with the Golden Arm*, a vigorous novel
about drug addiction that won the first National Book
Award in 1950 and was made into a successful movie starring Frank Sinatra. Money and fame were unable to go to
Nelson's resolutely nonconformist head; "down-at-the-
heel" would have been the politest term for the neighbor-
hood he still lived in, where he took the three of us (my
wife, Rose, having signed on at the last minute) after meeting our plane at O'Hare. It was a predominantly Polish
faubourg, hemmed in by mammoth gas-storage tanks, and
the odor of fatty sausage and cabbage began at the curb,
becoming more ripe and pronounced as we labored up the
five flights to what Nelson called his "penthouse"—an incredibly cramped and cluttered apartment with only two
small bedrooms, a tiny kitchenette, and an old-fashioned
bathroom with water-stained wallpaper.

The boxy living room was dark and jammed with
books. It was fairly clean amid the disorder, but the pad
was the lair of a totally undomesticated animal. I do recall

a framed photograph of Simone de Beauvoir, with whom Nelson had had a torrid affair, and whom he still referred to as "the Beaver." That night we partook of Polish cuisine, mystery stew and memorably awful, in a nearby restaurant, where Nelson titillated us with secret hints about the Chicago he was going to show us the next day. With the exception of Rose we all got pie-eyed. I was very fond of Nelson but I always thought he was half crazy. When he got enthusiastic or excited his eyes took on a manic gleam, and he would go off on a riff of giggles that was not unlike Richard Widmark's in *Kiss of Death*. Terry and I exchanged bewildered glances. I frankly had no idea what we would experience, thinking of such wonders as Michigan Avenue, the Art Institute, lunch at the Pump Room, the great Museum of Science and Industry, the Merchandise Mart, even the celebrated stockyards. That night, we three visitors slept in the same room, Rose and I locked immobile in a narrow, sagging single bed and Terry on a cot only a foot away, where he drifted off to sleep with a glass of bourbon still in his hand, heaving with laughter over Nelson and our accommodations.

Early the next morning, still behaving like a man withholding knowledge of a delightful mystery, Nelson took us by taxi on a meandering route through the city and deposited us at the entrance of the Cook County Jail. He then revealed that he had arranged to have us given a guided tour. This would be our most authentic taste of Chicago. We were all stunned—Terry, wearing his shades, said, "Well, Nelse old man, you shouldn't have gone to all the bother"—but in a way it was something I might have anticipated. Despite the merciless realism that he brought to his subject, Nelson was basically an underworld groupie; he loved all aspects of outlaw life, and his obsession with crime and criminals, though romantic, was eclectic to the extent that it also embraced the good guys. He counted among his many cronies a number of law enforcement officers, and one of these was the warden of the Cook County Jail. Despite the drab municipal sound of its name, the Cook County Jail was then, as now, a huge heavy-duty penitentiary, with harsh appurtenances such as a maximum-security unit, industrial areas, facilities for solitary confinement, and a thriving—if the term may be used—Death Row. All this was explained to us in his office by the warden, a thin man with a disarmingly scholarly look, whom Nelson introduced us to before vanishing—to our intense discomfort—saying he'd pick us up later. Clearly none of us could comprehend this sudden abandonment. While the warden fiddled with the buttons of his intercom, Terry wondered in a whisper if I was as hungover as he was; beneath his dark glasses his cheeks were sickly pale and I heard him murmur, "Man, I think this is turning into some kind of weird nightmare." Rose tried to appear happy and self-contained. We heard the warden summon Captain Boggs.

Captain Boggs had a round, cheerful, fudge-colored face and could not have weighed an ounce less than 250 pounds. His title was associate captain of the guards, and he would be our guide through the institution. As we trailed him down the corridor I couldn't help being struck by his extreme girth, which caused his arms to swing at wide angles from his body and made his body itself, beneath the slate-gray uniform jacket, appear somehow inflatable; he looked like a Negro version of the Michelin tire man. I was also fetched by his accent, with its rich loamy sound of the Deep South. I thought of Richard Wright's native son, Bigger Thomas, also an émigré from the cotton fields to Chicago, only to become the doomed murderer of a white girl; plainly Captain Boggs, in all of his heftiness, had made a prodigious leap for a onetime black boy. He had a rather deliberate and ornate manner of speaking, possibly the result of many trips with what he called "VIP honorees," and the tour itself dragged on through the prison's depressing immensity, seeming to continue hour after hour. "Dis yere is de inmates' dinin' facilities," he said as we stood on a balcony overlooking an empty mess hall. "Dis yere," he yelled at us at the doorway to a deafening machine shop, "is where de inmates pays off they debts to society." We went down into a cav-

ernous basement, chilly and echoing with a distant drip-
ping sound. "Dis yere is what is called de Hole. Solitary
confinement. You gits too smart, dis yere where you pays
fo' it." We would not be able to go on the tiers of the cell
blocks, Captain Boggs explained, Rose being a distracting
presence. "Dem suckers go wild aroun' a woman," he
declared.

We did end up, finally, on Death Row. After going
through a series of doors, we immediately entered a small,
windowless room, where we had a most disconcerting encounter. Seated at a table was a white inmate in orange
prison coveralls being given an intravenous injection by a
black male nurse. Captain Boggs introduced us to the pris-
oner, whose name was Witherspoon, a mountaineer trans-
plant up from Kentucky (and known in the press as "the
Hillbilly from Hell") who had committed a couple of particularly troglodytic murders in Chicago, and whose date
with the executioner was right around the corner. Witherspoon and his gruesome crimes were of national interest,
his case having made the New York papers.

"Howya doin', Witherspoon?" said Captain Boggs in a
hearty voice. "Dese is two writer gentlemen. Doin' de
VIP tour."

"Howdy," said Witherspoon, as he flashed a smile and
in so doing displayed a mouth full of blackened teeth in a
beetle-browed skeletal face that had doubtless inspired

many bad dreams. "I've got diabeet-ees," he went on to say, as if to explain the needle in his arm, and then, without missing a beat, added: "They done railroaded me. Before Almighty God, I'm an innocent man." Terry and I later recalled, while ensconced in the lounge car of the Super Chief, the almost hallucinatory sensations we both experienced when, most likely at the same time, we glimpsed the tattoos graven on Witherspoon's hands: LOVE on the fingers of the right hand, HATE on those of the left. They were exactly the mottoes that decorated the knuckles of Robert Mitchum's demented backwoods preacher in *The Night of the Hunter*. Witherspoon himself had a preacher's style. "I hope you two good writers will proclaim to the world the abominable injustice they done to me. God bless you both."

"Mr. Witherspoon," Terry deadpanned, "be assured of our constant concern for your welfare."

I had undergone a recent conversion about capital punishment, transformed from a believer—albeit a lukewarm believer—into an ardent opponent; hence my chagrin, after we bade good-bye to Witherspoon, when Captain Boggs walked us down a narrow corridor and acquainted us with the vehicle that would soon speed the Hillbilly from Hell back whence he came. We trooped into a sort of alcove where the captain motioned us to stand, while he went to one wall and yanked back a curtain. In glaring light there was suddenly revealed the electric chair, a huge hulking throne of wood and leather, out of which unraveled a thicket of wires. I heard Rose give a small soprano yelp of distress. In the lurid incandescence I noted on the far wall two signs. One read: SILENCE. The other: NO SMOKING. I felt Terry's paw on my shoulder, as from somewhere behind me he whispered: "Did you ever dig anything so fucking *surreal?*"

Captain Boggs said: "De supreme penalty." His voice slipped into the rhythmic rote-like monotone with which I was sure he had addressed countless VIP honorees. "De procedure is quick and painless. First is administered two thousand volts for thirty seconds. Stop de juice to let de body cool off. Den five hundred volts for thirty seconds. Stop de juice again. Den two thousand mo' volts. Doctor makes a final check. Ten minutes from beginnin' to end."

"Let me out of here," I heard Rose murmur.

"I always likes to ax de visitors if they'd care to set down in de chair," the captain said, his cheerful grin broadening. "How 'bout you, Mr. Starling?" he went on, using the name he'd called me by all morning.

I said that I'd pass on the offer, but I didn't want the opportunity lost on Terry. "What do you think, Tex?" I said.

"Captain Boggs," said Terry, "I've always wanted to experience the hot squat—vicariously, that is. But I think that today I'll decline your very tempting invitation."

I've recently discovered that the quite accurate notes I kept about our trip, which allow the foregoing account to possess verisimilitude, become rather sketchy after we leave the Cook County Jail. This is probably because our trip farther westward on the elegant Super Chief was largely a warm blur of booze and overeating, causing me to discontinue my notes except for a few random jottings, themselves nearly incoherent. (I want to mention, however, while the fact is fresh in mind, that some months after our trip I read that Witherspoon never had to receive that voltage; his death sentence was commuted, through a legal technicality, to life imprisonment.) I thought of Terry recently when I read, in an interview, the words of a British punk-rock star, plainly a young jerk, nasty and callow but able to express a tart intuitive insight: "You Americans still believe in God and all that shit, don't you? The whole fucking lot of you fraught with the fear of death."

Terry would have given his little cackle of approval at the remark, for it went to the core of his perception of American culture. Like me, Terry was an apostate southern Protestant, and I think that one of the reasons we hit it off well together was that we both viewed the Christian religion—at least insofar as we had experienced its puritanical rigors—as a conspiracy to deny its adherents their fulfillment as human beings. It magnified not the glories of life but the consciousness of death, exploiting humanity's innate terror of the timeless void. High among its prohibitions was sexual pleasure. In contemplating Americans stretched on the rack of their hypocrisy as they tried to reconcile their furtive adulteries with their churchgoing pieties, Terry laid the groundwork for some of his most biting and funniest satire. Christianity bugged him, even getting into his titles—think of *The Magic Christian*. Nor was it by chance that the surname of the endearing heroine of *Candy* was—what else?—Christian. His finest comic efforts often come from his juxtaposing a sweetly religious soul—or at least a bourgeois-conventional one—with a figure of depravity or corruption. *Candy* was surely the first novel in which the frenzied sexual congress between a well-bred, exquisitely proportioned young American girl and an elderly, insane hunchback could elicit nothing but helpless laughter. ("Give me your *hump!*" she squeals at the moment of climax, in a *jeu de mots* so obvious it compounds the hilarity.) One clear memory I have is of Terry in the lounge car, musing over his Old Grand-Dad as he considered the imminent demise of the Super Chief and, with it, a venerable tradition. His voice grew elegiac speaking of the number of "darling Baptist virgins aspiring to be starlets" who, at the hands of "panting Jewish agents with their swollen members," had been ever so satisfactorily deflowered on these plush, softly undulating banquettes.

In fact, he had a fixation on the idea of "starlets," and it was plain that in Hollywood he would be looking forward to making out with a gorgeous ingénue from MGM and embarking on a halcyon erotic adventure. Toward the end of the trip we stayed up all night and drank most of the way through Arizona and southern California, watching the pale moonscape of the desert slip by until morning dawned and we were in Los Angeles. Rose and I had to catch a late-morning plane to San Francisco but we all had time, it suddenly occurred to me, to visit the place that was the reason for Terry's trip. This was Forest Lawn Memorial Park, the "Whispering Glades" of Waugh's scathing send-up of America's funerary customs; how could Rose and I leave Los Angeles without viewing the hangout of Mr. Joyboy and his associate morticians? Terry agreed that we should all see it together. It was inevitable, I suppose, that the studio had arranged to put Terry up at that decaying relic the Chateau Marmont; for me it was an unexpected bonus to catch a glimpse of the mythic Hollywood landmark before heading out to Whispering Glades.

Terry and I were both in that sleepless state of jangled nerves and giggly mania, still half blotto and relying heavily on Rose and her sober patience to get us headed in the right direction. At Forest Lawn, in the blinding sunlight, our fellow tourists were out in droves. They were lined up in front of the mausoleum where the movie gods and goddesses had been laid to rest, stacked up in their crypts, Terry observed, "like pies in the Automat." Marilyn Monroe had passed into her estate of cosmic Loved One only two years before, and the queue of gawkers filing past her final abode seemed to stretch for hundreds of yards. Cameras clicked, bubble gum popped, babies shrieked. One sensed an awkward effort at reverence, but it was a strain; the spectacular graveyard was another outpost of Tinseltown. As we ambled over the greensward, vast as a golf course, we moved past a particularly repellent statuary grouping, a tableau of mourning marble children and a clutch of small marble animals. A woman onlooker was gushing feverishly, and Terry said he felt a little ill. We all agreed to be on our separate ways. "A bit of shut-eye and I'll soon be in tip-top shape," he assured us as we embraced. We left him standing at the taxi stop. He had his hands thrust deep in his pockets, and he was scowling through his shades, looking fierce and, as always, a little confused and lost but, in any case, with the mammoth American necropolis as a backdrop, like a man already dreaming up wicked ideas.

—*The Paris Review,* SPRING 1996

A LITERARY FOREFATHER

H E IS MY MOST BELOVED LITERARY FOREFATHER, but it's not just my affection for *Adventures of Huckleberry Finn* that makes me feel close to Mark Twain. Our other affinities continually surprise me. Although a century, minus a decade, separates our birth dates, we had curiously similar upbringings. Mark Twain's border South and my Tidewater Virginia shared the burden of a sullen racism, even though the functional slavery of Hannibal, Missouri, had been in my case replaced by the bitter pseudoslavery of Jim Crow; both left imprints on a white boy's soul. Plainly it affected Mark Twain that the Clemens family had been slaveholders; I was haunted (and am still amazed) by the reality that my grandmother, an old lady still alive in the mid-1930s, had owned slaves as a little girl. Our early surroundings possessed a surface sweetness and innocence—under which lay a turmoil we were pleased to expose—and we both grew up in villages on the banks of great rivers that dominated our lives.

The muddy James was an essential presence in my boyhood ("It was a monstrous big river down there," says Huck of the Mississippi as he and Jim drift southward, "sometimes a mile and a half wide"; my James River was *five* miles wide), and the edgy relationship I had with black children was identical to that of Mark Twain. "All the negroes were friends of ours, and with those of our own age we were in effect comrades," he wrote in his autobiography. "We were comrades, and yet not comrades; color and condition interposed a subtle line which both parties were conscious of and which rendered complete fusion impossible." This near paralysis of affection (which has such a modern resonance) remained as true for me in my Tidewater village as it had been for Mark Twain in Hannibal, and worked on both of us its psychological mischief. In our later lives Mark Twain and I chose to dwell among Connecticut Yankees (during years interrupted by sojourns as Innocents Abroad), and it was there, bedeviled by our pasts, that we wrote books about slavery called *Huckleberry Finn* and *The Confessions of Nat Turner*. Both of these novels gained indisputable success and a multitude of readers but, because they dealt with America's most profound dilemma—its racial anguish—in ways that were idiosyncratic and upsetting, and because they contained many ambiguities, they invited the wrath of critics, black and white, in controversies that have persisted to this day.

As for *Huckleberry Finn*, it's quite likely that if Mark Twain had merely used "slave" instead of the word "nigger," which appears more than two hundred times during the course of the narrative, many of those who have recently attacked the book on the grounds of racism would have been at least partially appeased. But "nigger," our most powerful secular blasphemy—now that virtually all crude sexual expressions have become part of public speech, melded into the monotonous jawing of stage, screen, and cable TV—still has a scary force. Huck Finn's use of it, especially in these touchy years, has driven some people around the bend. Although a twelve-year-old Missourian would have had scant familiarity, in the 1840s, with the word "slave"—a term that was generally confined to governmental proclamations, religious discussions, and legal documents—Huck's innocent vernacular usage appears to be one of the reasons for the panic that recently impelled the Cathedral School of Washington, D.C., of all esteemed institutions, to remove *Huckleberry Finn* from its tenth-grade curriculum. Only the nature of the school surprises; over the past decades the book has been banished from library shelves innumerable times.

Even more incoherent is the activity of a black educator from Fairfax, Virginia, named John H. Wallace. With some success, Wallace has campaigned to protect youth from the bad word by insisting that *Huckleberry Finn* be taken away from school libraries, and has published what has to be an all time curiosity in the annals of bowdlerization: a version of the text from which every use of the word "nigger" has been expunged. The crusade of Wallace, who has described his nemesis as "the most grotesque example of racist trash ever written," might be considered merely a spectacular eccentricity if it weren't a fairly menacing example of the animus that has always coalesced around the novel. Not that the book is beyond criticism. It has been charged that *Huckleberry Finn* reveals the mind of a writer with equivocal feelings about race, and signs to that effect may certainly be found. The wonder is that his upbringing and experience (including a brief stint in the Confederate army) should have left Mark Twain so little tainted with bigotry. Although most of its millions of readers, including many black people, have found no racism in the book (Ralph Ellison wrote admiringly of the author's grasp of the tormented complexity of slavery, his awareness of Jim's essential humanity), *Huckleberry Finn* has never really struggled up out of a continuous vortex of discord, and probably never will as long as its enchanting central figures, with their confused and incalculable feelings for each other, remain symbols of our own racial confusion.

As I reflect on the kinship I have always felt with Mark Twain, I am reminded that no American rivers are so bound up with the history of slavery as are the Mississippi and the James. As a boy I had learned that our own slavery began on the James, in 1619; I sometimes had vivid fantasies in which I would see, far out in the channel, that first small clumsy Dutch galleon beating its way upriver to Jamestown, with its cargo of miserable black people in chains. For me the river meant stifling bondage. For Mark Twain, writing after the Civil War, the Mississippi, and the uproarious, extravagant voyage he launched upon it, meant freedom—not merely freedom for Jim but a nation's freedom from the primal ache that had racked its soul ever since Jamestown. It's a measure of *Huckleberry Finn*'s greatness, but also perhaps of the insufficiency of the relief it has given us from pain, that it still receives such savage attacks. The pain continues. Let the attacks continue, too. They will only prove the durability of a work that has withstood the complaints of boors and puritans, and will surely weather the blows of this grim and dogmatic time.

—*The New Yorker*, 26 JUNE–3 JULY 1995
(originally published in a shorter form)

SLAVERY'S PAIN,
DISNEY'S GAIN

I MAGINEERING, AN ADROIT NEOLOGISM, IS THE WALT Disney Company's name for the corporate unit involved in developing Disney's America, the projected mammoth theme park in northern Virginia. Not long ago, the chief imagineer, Robert Weis, described what would be in store, among other historical attractions for hordes of tourists. "We want to make you feel what it was like to be a slave, and what it was like to escape through the Underground Railroad." He added that the exhibits would "not take a Pollyanna view" but would be "painful, disturbing and agonizing."

I was fascinated by Mr. Weis's statement because twenty-seven years ago I published a novel called *The Confessions of Nat Turner*, which was partly intended to make the reader feel what it was like to be a slave. Whether I succeeded or not was a matter of hot debate, and the book still provokes controversy. But as one who has plunged into the murky waters where the imagineers wish to venture, I have doubts whether the technical wizardry that so entrances children and grown-ups at other Disney parks can do anything but mock a theme as momentous as slavery, the great transforming circumstance of American history. If it is so difficult to render the tragic complexity of slavery in words, as I once found out, will visual effects or virtual reality make it easier to comprehend the agony?

No one knows what Disney's Department of Imagineering has up its sleeve, but whatever exhibits or displays it comes up with would have to be fraudulent, since no combination of branding irons, slave ships or slave cabins, shackles, chained black people in their wretched coffles, or treks through the Underground Railroad could begin to define such a stupendous experience. To present even the most squalid sights would be to cheaply romanticize suffering. For slavery's abyssal pain arose far less from its physical cruelty—although slave ships and the auction block were atrocities—than from the moral and legal savagery that deprived an entire people of their freedom, along with their rights to education, ownership of property, matrimony, and protection under the law.

Slavery cannot be represented by exhibits. It was not remotely like the Jewish Holocaust—of brief duration and intensely focused destruction—which has permitted an illuminating museum. In its 250-year history in America, the institution, which so intimately bound slave and master together, could not fail to produce almost unlimited permutations of human emotions and relationships. How would the Disney technicians make millions of their pilgrims feel all these things? How would they show that there were white people who suffered torment over the catastrophe? And how can they possibly render, beyond the deafening noise and the nasty gore, the infinitely subtle moral entanglements of the terrible war that brought slavery to an end?

I was born and reared in Virginia, and I am the grandson of a slave owner. I continue to be astonished that in the waning years of the twentieth century, I should possess a flesh-and-blood link with the remote past—that from boyhood I have a luminous memory of an old lady, my grandmother, who actually owned black slaves. For this very reason, she has haunted my life, become embedded in the fabric of my work as a writer, and helped make slavery an undiminishing part of my consciousness. Her story, some of which I recall being told in her own quavering and stubborn voice, would possess no appeal for those planning the wicked frisson of a Simon Legree tableau, but it has its own harrowing truth.

The drama began in 1863, the year the Emancipation Proclamation was issued, when Union troops occupied much of eastern Virginia and part of northeastern North

Carolina. That spring, my grandmother, Marianna Clark, was a twelve-year-old living on a remote plantation where her father owned thirty-five slaves. Two of the slaves were girls, roughly her age, who had been given to her by deed. She had grown up with them and played with them; they had become so lovingly close that, not surprisingly, the children regarded one another as sisters. Her clearest memory was of having knitted woolen stockings for the girls during that bitter winter.

One morning, a large body of Union cavalrymen, detached from General Ambrose Burnside's forces, swept down on the plantation, stripped it bare of everything valuable and worthless, edible and movable, burned down the outbuildings, and, after a day's long plunder, disappeared. Most of the slaves departed with the troops, and the little girls also vanished. My grandmother never saw them again. She and the family verged close to starvation for several months, forced "to chew roots and eat rats." She grieved for the girls but her grief may have been absorbed into her own suffering, for she became a near skeleton, and the deprivation, I suspect, arrested her growth, making her diminutive and weak-boned (though she was amazingly resilient) to the end of her long life.

My grandmother's terror and trauma were genuine, but they have to be reckoned as no great matter in the end, for she survived the privation of Reconstruction, reared six children in reasonable comfort, and died at eighty-seven, at peace except for her feeling about Yankees, for whom she had a fund of inexhaustible rage and contempt. What has haunted me is those slave girls, her "little sisters" who vanished on that spring day and caused her to mourn whenever she spoke of them. One can be certain that they had no easy time of it. Swallowed up into the legion of disfranchised ex-slaves, they had little to look forward to in the oncoming years of poverty, the Ku Klux Klan, a storm of hatred, joblessness, illiteracy, lynchings, and the suffocating night of Jim Crow. They were truly, in the lament of the spiritual, among the "many thousand gone."

This renewed bondage is the collective anguish from which white Americans have always averted their eyes. And it underlines the falseness of any Disneyesque rendition of slavery. The falseness is in the assumption that by viewing the artifacts of cruelty and oppression, or whatever the imagineers cook up—the cabins, the chains, the auction block—one will have succumbed in a "disturbing and agonizing" manner to the catharsis of a completed tragedy. But the drama has never ended. At Disney's Virginia park, the slave experience would permit visitors a shudder of horror before they turned away, smug and self-exculpatory, from a world that may be dead but has not really been laid to rest.

—*The New York Times* (Op-Ed), 4 AUGUST 1994

TOO LATE FOR
CONVERSION OR PRAYER

I MUST SPEAK OF MY FAVORITE PILL IN THE PERSPEC-
tive of Christian theology. In order to explain this connection I shall have to include some intimate personal details
that I hope will not offend sensitive readers.

A number of years ago I got into a friendly but spirited
argument with the Episcopal bishop of New York, whom
I encountered at a party on Martha's Vineyard. We were
discussing the existence of God. I declared to the bishop
that the nonexistence of God could be proved by the existence of the prostate gland. The bishop, a liberal, had been
describing Darwinian evolution as the product of "God's
divine wisdom." No wise God, I countered, could have let
evolve a biological species, such as *Homo sapiens*, in which
any organ so stupid, so faulty, so prone to disease and dys-
function as the prostate gland had been allowed to exist.
Ergo: if God did exist, he certainly was not wise. The as-
sembled guests, who were listening to our discussion,

applauded me—at least the men did—but the argument went unresolved.

Some years after this meeting, when I began to experience prostate trouble, I wondered if I might not have courted the wrath of God through my contemptuous skepticism. Maybe the bishop was right. It could be that God did exist, after all, and it was disbelievers like me whom he punished most exultantly by wreaking havoc on their prostate glands. I thought about expressing contrition, but the seriousness of my symptoms convinced me that it was too late for conversion or prayer.

When a man begins to have prostate trouble he experiences difficulties with his plumbing. The problem is often idiosyncratic, varying from man to man, but it almost always involves aberrant behavior of the bladder. Sometimes a man will feel the urgent need to urinate many times a day, discovering that each time he goes to the bathroom he passes only a small amount of urine. Sometimes the flow is not steady, sometimes it is weak; often one has to push or strain to begin urination. All of these difficulties are the result of a usually benign condition in which the enlarged prostate encroaches on the urethra.

In my own case the most serious manifestations occurred at night, when the call to urinate forced me to get up almost every hour. Such an irregular sleeping pattern began to create in me severe exhaustion. More seriously, however, I discovered that my flow was beginning to shut down almost completely. One morning at dawn I realized to my horror that I couldn't urinate at all. I had to be driven to the emergency room of the hospital, where I was relieved of my distress by a catheter inserted into my blad der. It was my birthday. You may imagine the revolting self-pity I felt at celebrating that day as I shuffled around hesitantly with a tube stuck up my penis and a plastic bag attached to my leg.

Of course, I went to a urologist immediately. The doctor examined me carefully and determined that I didn't have cancer. This was a great relief, but then he said that I might have to submit to a surgical procedure to relieve the symptoms. I asked him to describe the operation. He told me jovially that, because the procedure resembled the technique used to ream out sewer pipes, it was often called the "Roto-Rooter." A long instrument with a blade at the end was inserted up through the penis, and portions of the prostate gland were shaved off; this allowed the return of the urine flow, and the patient began to function normally. Well, *almost* normally, the doctor said after a pause. I asked him to explain.

There were side effects to be expected, he went on. The most common complication had to do with sexual function. The capacity for orgasm was usually retained, although, he added, a bit hesitantly, some men felt diminished pleasure. More significant, however, was the nature of the ejaculation. He then described a process so bizarre that I scarcely believed it, but it happens to be true. In the majority of cases, the semen was propelled not forward in the usual fashion but backward into the bladder, where it was eliminated through urination. Would this cause one's partner, I wondered, to whisper not "Have you come, darling?" but "Have you gone?" At any rate, as he described this process, known as "retrograde ejaculation," I began to feel faint. Although the majority of the operations had no seriously negative aftermath, he continued, he felt it was his duty to tell me that, in a few cases, there were complications. I again asked him to elaborate. Some men were left impotent, he said, with no erectile function. What else? I inquired. A small number of patients suffered permanent urinary incontinence, requiring the daily use of diapers.

By this time I was sobbing uncontrollably, but inside, so the doctor couldn't see.

Then his expression brightened. Surgery should of course be avoided if possible, and he wanted me to try a new pill that had just been made available to urologists. Although it was not yet approved by the Food and Drug Administration, many urologists had achieved great success in preliminary tests. Originally intended as a medication to lower blood pressure, it was discovered to have the property of relaxing the muscles at the bladder outlet. The doctor urged me to take the pills home and see if they worked.

Dear reader, to make a long story short, a miracle happened. The pill worked magnificently. For the past five years I have been taking one small five-milligram dose nightly, and my flow has been like Niagara. There have been no side effects. I did not have to have that Roto-Rooter. I do not have to wear diapers. I am not impotent. My semen does not go backward but still spurts out merrily in the direction Nature intended. I am at peace with my genitourinary system and with the world. The pill is a true wonder drug, which demonstrates for me that if the bishop of New York was right and God exists, and that if he is trying to punish men by way of their prostate glands, we have triumphantly outwitted him.

— Egoïste 7 (1985)

THE WANAMAKER DIARY

Friday
19

After April 1900
Edgar + I started
to work on the
boat but we were
rained out. After
supper Pop went get
calling and I went
to see "Invisible Stripes"
at the Paramount.
retty good. to bed.

Saturday
20

In the morning I
painted, or "topsided
up" the boat. I
also helped Pop in
the yard. Went up the
stores, and then helped
Joe Mitchell on his
boat down at the river.
Pop and I had supper at the
Cafeteria. I
took his treatment at Dr.

ORIGINS OF ETIQUETTE (4)—The hope chest. The hope chest grew out of
the custom of marriage by purchase. Later brides had dowries, and out of this has
come the modern custom of the bride-to-be starting a hope chest.

Knowles, and we went to
see "My Little Chickadee"
Very good. to bed.

William Styron's Wanamaker Diary for 19–20 April 1940 (he was fourteen years old). The movies are Invisible Stripes, *a 1939 crime drama with George Raft and Humphrey Bogart, and the 1940 classic* My Little Chickadee, *starring W. C. Fields and Mae West.*

MOVIEGOER

FOR SEVEN OR EIGHT MONTHS DURING MY FOUR-teenth year I kept a diary. This was in the late 1930s, when I was living in southern Virginia with my father and a male cousin a little older than I—my mother having died a year before. Because of the absence of my mother there was considerably less discipline in the household than there ordinarily might have been, and so the diary—which I still possess—is largely a chronicle of idleness. The only interruptions to appear amid the daily inertia are incidents of moviegoing. The diary now records the fact that hardly a day went by without my cousin and me at-tending a film, and on weekends we often went more than once. In the summertime, when we had no school, there was a period of ten days when we viewed a total of sixteen movies. Mercifully, it must be recorded, movies were very cheap during those years at the end of the Great Depres-sion. My critical comments in the diary were invariably laconic: "Pretty good." "Not bad." "Really swell movie." I was fairly undemanding in my tastes. The purely negative remarks are almost nonexistent.

Among the several remarkable features about this orgy of moviegoing there is one that stands out notably: nowhere during this brief history is there even the slightest mention of my having read a book. As far as reading was concerned, I may as well have been an illiterate sharecropper in Alabama. So one might ask: how does a young boy, exposed so numbingly and monotonously to a single medium—the film—grow up to become a writer of fiction? The answer, I believe, may be less complicated than one might suppose. In the first place, I would like to think that, if my own experience forms an example, it does not mean the deaths of literacy or creativity if one is drenched in popular culture at an early age. This is not to argue in favor of such a witless exposure to movies as I have just described—only to say that the very young probably survive such exposure better than we imagine, and grow up to be readers and writers. More importantly, I think my experience demonstrates how, at least in the last fifty or sixty years, it has been virtually impossible for a writer of fiction to be immune to the influence of film on his work, or to fail to have movies impinge in an important way on his creative consciousness.

Yet I need to make an immediate qualification. I do not

wish to argue matters of superiority in art forms. But although I cannot be entirely objective, I must say here that as admirable and as powerful a medium as the cinema is, it cannot achieve that complex synthesis of poetic, intellectual, and emotional impact that we find in the very finest novels. At their best, films are of course simply wonderful. A work like *Citizen Kane* or *The Treasure of the Sierra Madre* (by one of the greatest of directors, John Huston, who, interestingly enough, began his career as a writer) is each infinitely superior, in my opinion, to most novels aspiring to the status of literature. But neither of these estimable works attains for me the aesthetic intensity of, say, William Faulkner in a book like *The Sound and the Fury*, or comes close to the profound beauty and moral vision of the novel that, more than any other, determined my early course as a writer: *Madame Bovary*.

After saying this, however, I feel obliged to confess without apology to the enormous influence the cinema has had on my own writing. Here I am not speaking of films in any large sense contributing to my philosophical understanding of things; even the films of Ingmar Bergman and Luis Buñuel, both of whom I passionately admire, fail to achieve that synthesis I mentioned before. While a fine movie has changed my perceptions for days, a great novel has altered my way of thinking for life. No, what I am speaking of is technique, style, mood—the manner in which remembered episodes in films, certain attitudes and gestures on the part of actors, little directorial tricks, even echoes of dialogue have infiltrated my work.

I am not by nature a creature of the eye (in the sense that I respond acutely to painting or pictorial representation; I vibrate instead to music) but I'm certain that the influence of films has caused my work to be intensely visual. I clearly recollect much of the composition of my first novel, *Lie Down in Darkness,* which I finished when I was twenty-five. So many scenes from that book were set up in my mind as I might have set them up as a director. My authorial eye became a camera, and the page became a set or soundstage upon which my characters entered or exited and spoke their lines as if from a script. This is a dramatic technique that by no means necessarily diminishes the literary integrity of a novel; it is, as I say, a happy legacy of many years of moviegoing, and it has resonance still in my latest work, *Sophie's Choice*. For example, I wrote the scene toward the end of the film where Stingo ascends the stairs in the rooming house to view the dead bodies of Sophie and Nathan with such an overpowering sense of viewing it through the eyepiece of a movie camera that when I saw the episode re-created in the film I had a stunning sense of déjà vu, as if I myself had photographed the scene, directed it, rather than written it in a book.

Indeed, the film version of *Sophie's Choice* gives me an

excellent opportunity to sum up my attitudes toward the relationship between literature and the cinema. Alan Pakula's production is, I think, a remarkably faithful adaptation of the novel, the kind of interpretation that every writer of novels ideally longs for but almost never receives. When I first saw the film it was a joy to note the smooth, almost seamless way the story unfolded in scrupulous fidelity to the way I had told it; there were no shortcuts, no distortions or evasions, and the sense of satisfaction I felt was augmented by the splendid photography, the subtle musical score, and, above all, the superb acting, especially Meryl Streep's glorious performance, which of course is already part of film history. What then, when it was all over, was the cause of my nagging uneasiness, the sense that something was missing?

Suddenly I realized that much that had been essential to the novel had been quietly eliminated, so much that I could scarcely catalog the vanished items: the important digression on racial conflict, the philosophical meditations on Auschwitz, the intense eroticism between Sophie and Nathan, the exploration of anti-Semitism in Poland, even certain characters I had considered crucial to the novel— these were but a few of the aspects which were gone. Yet in no sense did I feel betrayed. After calm reflection I understood the necessity for the absence of these components: many things had to go; otherwise a ten-hour film would have ensued. But more significantly, those elements which had been so carefully integrated into the novel, and which were so important both to its execution and to that sense of density and complicity which makes a novel the special organism it is, were those which most likely would have ruined the film had there been an attempt to include them.

Thus the film had to be not a visual replica of the novel—such was impossible—but a skeleton upon which was hung only the merest suggestion of the novel's flesh. For me it illustrated more graphically than anything the necessity for not expecting a film to perform a novel's work. The two art forms—basically so different—coexist but rarely achieve a coupling. At best, a film (like *Sophie's Choice*) can take on a felicitous resemblance, as in a fine translation of a poem from a difficult language. And that is no small achievement. But even the most satisfied moviemaker will say, if he is honest, that for the true experience one must return to that oldest source—the written word—and confront the original work.

—*Le Figaro,* 7–8 MAY 1983

FESSING UP

I WAS A MEMBER OF THE ENTIRELY WHITE, PREDOMI-
nantly male, and somewhat doddering Modern Library
editorial board that compiled a list of the hundred best
novels written in English in the twentieth century. I don't
want to dodge my contribution to the list's notoriety. In
fact, I want to cheerfully assent to the opinion expressed in
these pages that the list is "weird." When I saw the final
roster, I was a little shocked at what the ten of us had
wrought, not only in respect to the list's glaring omissions
(no Toni Morrison, no Patrick White, only eight women
in the lot) but in respect to its generally oppressive stodginess. The voting process was partly at fault for this quality
of desuetude. A luncheon meeting with a good wine that
allowed for lively disputation would have soon eliminated
such toothless pretenders as *The Magnificent Ambersons*
and *Zuleika Dobson*.

As it was, we voted by mail ballot. Each judge checked

①

(Grace: surround book titles with quotation marks)

I was a member of the entirely white, predominantly male and somewhat doddering Modern Library editorial board that compiled a list of the one hundred best novels written in English in the twentieth century, and I cheerfully assent to Louis Menand's opinion expressed in this magazine, that the list is "weird." When I saw the final roster I was a little shocked at what the ten of us had wrought, not only in respect to the list glaring omissions (no Toni Morrison, no Patrick White only nine women in the lot) but to its generally oppressive stodginess. The voting process was partly at fault for this quality of deadwood. A luncheon meeting with good wine that allowed for lively disputation would have soon eliminated such toothless preferenda as "The Magnificent Ambersons" and "Zuleika Dobson." As it was, we voted by mail ballot. Each judge checked off from a roll call of several hundred novels the works he (or in the case of A. S. Byatt, she) thought worthy of making the cut. The books were then ranked by number of votes tallied, those receiving, say, nine votes (like "Ulysses" and "The Great Gatsby") were placed at the top of the list and the others were rated downward accordingly. That Aldous Huxley's "Brave New World" and Samuel Butler's "The Way of All Flesh"

The first page of Styron's manuscript for "Fessing Up."

off from a roll call of several hundred novels the works he (or, in the case of A. S. Byatt, she) thought worthy of making the cut. The books were then ranked by the number of the votes tallied. Those receiving, say, nine votes (like *Ulysses* and *The Great Gatsby*) were placed at the top of the list, and the others were rated downward accordingly. Such a procedure led to some odd (or weird) results. That Aldous Huxley's *Brave New World* and Samuel Butler's *The Way of All Flesh* reached the empyrean (at Nos. 5 and 12, respectively) didn't necessarily mean they deserved such an exalted rating. It meant only that eight or nine judges just happened to believe those books belonged somewhere among the anointed hundred.

People who were legitimately exasperated by the Modern Library's inventory might take heart from a rival list drawn up by the bright members of the course in publishing at Radcliffe College, and printed in the *Boston Globe* and *USA Today*, among other papers. They would be encouraged, at least at first, by the youth of those involved (most are in their twenties) and by the fact that most are female and some nonwhite. The students' choices, while often extravagant, are in many cases a bracing corrective to the Modern Library's pervasive air of superannuation. An example: *The Catcher in the Rye*, bogged down at No. 64 on our list, vaults to second place, right after *The Great Gatsby*.

In a way, the Radcliffe list is as proper and predictable as the Modern Library's. It pays appropriate homage to the great modernist authors: Joyce, Faulkner, Hemingway, Woolf, Steinbeck, James, Orwell, Nabokov. Yet it also affirms the importance of certain women writers not present on the other list, notably Toni Morrison (with three titles) and Flannery O'Connor. Sometimes the importance is exaggerated: Alice Walker's *The Color Purple* at No. 5? But most of the old fogies to whom one might rightly object have been dumped: Booth Tarkington, Arnold Bennett, James T. Farrell, Thornton Wilder, and John O'Hara. These patricides seem to be worthy ones, allowing space not only for writers whose absence was conspicuous from the Modern Library list—John Updike and Don DeLillo—but for a small yet refreshing category: children's books.

They seemed a wonderful addition. I found myself not giving a damn that *Charlotte's Web* (No. 13) and *Winnie-the-Pooh* (No. 22) were in a much loftier position than *A Passage to India* (No. 59) and *Sons and Lovers* (No. 64). But I began to be made uneasy by the realization that many significant gains were offset by inexplicable losses. Where was the matchless Graham Greene? What happened to Saul Bellow and Philip Roth? Walker Percy's *The Moviegoer* was gone, as was John Cheever's *The Wapshot Chronicle*; and who should pop up in their stead but the hectoring

Ayn Rand, represented by her dismal blockbusters *The Fountainhead* and *Atlas Shrugged*.

Moreover, just as the Modern Library list had done, the Radcliffe list ignored virtually all experimental fiction and many widely read contemporaries—from Beckett to Pynchon, from Joan Didion to Robert Stone. Finally, there were the profoundly eccentric rankings. Is Douglas Adams's *The Hitchhiker's Guide to the Galaxy* really better than anything written by Theodore Dreiser?

Somewhere in this is a lesson. Perhaps it's only that all lists are weird, but each list is weird in its own way.

—*The New Yorker*, 17 AUGUST 1998

Have You Read the 100 Best Novels of the 20th Century?

❑ 1. **Ulysses**, James Joyce*
❑ 2. **The Great Gatsby**, F. Scott Fitzgerald
❑ 3. **A Portrait Of The Artist As A Young Man**, James Joyce*
❑ 4. **Lolita**, Vladimir Nabokov
❑ 5. **Brave New World**, Aldous Huxley
❑ 6. **The Sound And The Fury**, William Faulkner*
❑ 7. **Catch-22**, Joseph Heller
❑ 8. **Darkness At Noon**, Arthur Koestler
❑ 9. **Sons And Lovers**, D. H. Lawrence*
❑ 10. **The Grapes Of Wrath**, John Steinbeck
❑ 11. **Under The Volcano**, Malcolm Lowry
❑ 12. **The Way Of All Flesh**, Samuel Butler*
❑ 13. **1984**, George Orwell
❑ 14. **I, Claudius**, Robert Graves
❑ 15. **To The Lighthouse**, Virginia Woolf
❑ 16. **An American Tragedy**, Theodore Dreiser
❑ 17. **The Heart Is A Lonely Hunter**, Carson McCullers*
❑ 18. **Slaughterhouse-Five**, Kurt Vonnegut
❑ 19. **Invisible Man**, Ralph Ellison*
❑ 20. **Native Son**, Richard Wright
❑ 21. **Henderson The Rain King**, Saul Bellow
❑ 22. **Appointment In Samarra**, John O'Hara*
❑ 23. **U.S.A.(Trilogy)**, John Dos Passos
❑ 24. **Winesburg, Ohio**, Sherwood Anderson*
❑ 25. **A Passage To India**, E. M. Forster
❑ 26. **The Wings Of The Dove**, Henry James*
❑ 27. **The Ambassadors**, Henry James
❑ 28. **Tender Is The Night**, F. Scott Fitzgerald
❑ 29. **The Studs Lonigan Trilogy**, James T. Farrell
❑ 30. **The Good Soldier**, Ford Madox Ford
❑ 31. **Animal Farm**, George Orwell
❑ 32. **The Golden Bowl**, Henry James
❑ 33. **Sister Carrie**, Theodore Dreiser*
❑ 34. **A Handful Of Dust**, Evelyn Waugh
❑ 35. **As I Lay Dying**, William Faulkner
❑ 36. **All The King's Men**, Robert Penn Warren
❑ 37. **The Bridge Of San Luis Rey**, Thornton Wilder
❑ 38. **Howards End**, E. M. Forster*
❑ 39. **Go Tell It On The Mountain**, James Baldwin*
❑ 40. **The Heart Of The Matter**, Graham Greene
❑ 41. **Lord Of The Flies**, William Golding
❑ 42. **Deliverance**, James Dickey
❑ 43. **A Dance To The Music Of Time (Series)**, Anthony Powell
❑ 44. **Point Counter Point**, Aldous Huxley
❑ 45. **The Sun Also Rises**, Ernest Hemingway
❑ 46. **The Secret Agent**, Joseph Conrad*
❑ 47. **Nostromo**, Joseph Conrad*
❑ 48. **The Rainbow**, D. H. Lawrence

❑ 49. **Women In Love**, D. H. Lawrence
❑ 50. **Tropic Of Cancer**, Henry Miller
❑ 51. **The Naked And The Dead**, Norman Mailer
❑ 52. **Portnoy's Complaint**, Philip Roth
❑ 53. **Pale Fire**, Vladimir Nabokov
❑ 54. **Light In August**, William Faulkner
❑ 55. **On The Road**, Jack Kerouac
❑ 56. **The Maltese Falcon**, Dashiell Hammett
❑ 57. **Parade's End**, Ford Madox Ford
❑ 58. **The Age Of Innocence**, Edith Wharton*
❑ 59. **Zuleika Dobson**, Max Beerbohm*
❑ 60. **The Moviegoer**, Walker Percy
❑ 61. **Death Comes For The Archbishop**, Willa Cather*
❑ 62. **From Here To Eternity**, James Jones
❑ 63. **The Wapshot Chronicle**, John Cheever
❑ 64. **The Catcher In The Rye**, J. D. Salinger
❑ 65. **A Clockwork Orange**, Anthony Burgess
❑ 66. **Of Human Bondage**, W. Somerset Maugham*
❑ 67. **Heart Of Darkness**, Joseph Conrad*
❑ 68. **Main Street**, Sinclair Lewis*
❑ 69. **The House Of Mirth**, Edith Wharton*
❑ 70. **The Alexandria Quartet**, Lawrence Durrell
❑ 71. **A High Wind In Jamaica**, Richard Hughes
❑ 72. **A House For Mr Biswas**, V. S. Naipaul
❑ 73. **The Day Of The Locust**, Nathanael West*
❑ 74. **A Farewell To Arms**, Ernest Hemingway
❑ 75. **Scoop**, Evelyn Waugh
❑ 76. **The Prime Of Miss Jean Brodie**, Muriel Spark
❑ 77. **Finnegans Wake**, James Joyce
❑ 78. **Kim**, Rudyard Kipling
❑ 79. **A Room With A View**, E. M. Forster*
❑ 80. **Brideshead Revisited**, Evelyn Waugh
❑ 81. **The Adventures Of Augie March**, Saul Bellow
❑ 82. **Angle Of Repose**, Wallace Stegner
❑ 83. **A Bend In The River**, V. S. Naipaul*
❑ 84. **The Death Of The Heart**, Elizabeth Bowen
❑ 85. **Lord Jim**, Joseph Conrad
❑ 86. **Ragtime**, E. L. Doctorow*
❑ 87. **The Old Wives' Tale**, Arnold Bennett
❑ 88. **The Call Of The Wild**, Jack London*
❑ 89. **Loving**, Henry Green
❑ 90. **Midnight's Children**, Salman Rushdie
❑ 91. **Tobacco Road**, Erskine Caldwell
❑ 92. **Ironweed**, William Kennedy
❑ 93. **The Magus**, John Fowles*
❑ 94. **Wide Sargasso Sea**, Jean Rhys
❑ 95. **Under The Net**, Iris Murdoch
❑ 96. **Sophie's Choice**, William Styron*
❑ 97. **The Sheltering Sky**, Paul Bowles
❑ 98. **The Postman Always Rings Twice**, James M. Cain
❑ 99. **The Ginger Man**, J. P. Donleavy
❑ 100. **The Magnificent Ambersons**, Booth Tarkington*

Published, or soon to be published, by the Modern Library

MODERN LIBRARY 100 BEST NOVELS
www.randomhouse.com/modernlibrary

The Modern Library list of the 100 best fiction books of the century (1998). For other book lists generated in the controversy, including the Radcliffe list, go to http://www.randomhouse.com/modernlibrary/100bestnovels.html.

WALKING WITH AQUINNAH

For the last four or five years, whenever I am home—which has been most of the time—I have been accustomed to taking long daily walks with my dog, Aquinnah. Our walks are for business and pleasure, and also for survival—interlocking motives that have somehow acquired nearly equal importance in my mind. From the professional point of view, there is nothing better than walking at a brisk pace to force oneself into a contemplative mood. I say force because there is, I'm sorry to relate, an early resistance. I am not by nature a very active person and it's a little embarrassing to confess that after many years of walking, with all sorts of dogs that preceded Aquinnah, it still takes at least a mild act of will to get started on my daily journey. For unlike most purely athletic activities, there is at the outset an element of joylessness in the walking process.

Strange that this is so. It requires absolutely no skill

save the natural one that we all acquire at infancy. Why should the mere act of consecutively putting one foot ahead of the other for mile after mile be in itself so unpleasant an idea as to inspire a reluctance still difficult for me to surmount? But once I get myself going there always comes a breakthrough, after the boredom that usually envelops me like a dank mist during the first quarter of a mile or so of my hike. At the start it is like a faint palpable ache, not in the feet or legs but somewhere around the rim of the cranium. I wonder why, once again, I am engaging in this ponderous movement. My mind is cluttered by a series of the most dismally mundane preoccupations: my bank balance, a dental appointment, the electrician's failure to come and repair a critical outlet. Invariably the first five or ten minutes are filled with sour musings—a splendid time to recollect old slights and disappointments and grudges, all flitting in and out of my consciousness like evil little goblins. They are the grimy bits and pieces of the initial boredom.

Yet almost without fail there comes a transitional moment—somewhat blurred, like that drowsy junction between wakefulness and sleep—when I begin to think of my work, when the tiny worries and injustices that have besieged me start to evaporate, replaced by a delicious, isolated contemplation of whatever is in the offing, later that day, at the table at which I write. Ideas, conceits, characters, even whole sentences and parts of paragraphs come pouring in on me in a happy flood until I am in a state close to hypnosis, quite oblivious of the woods or the fields or the beach where I am trudging, and finally as heedless of the rhythmic motion of my feet as if I were paddling through air like some great liberated goose or swan.

This, you see, is the delight and the value of walking for a writer. The writer lounging—trying to think, to sort out his thoughts—cannot really think, being the prey of endless distractions. He gets up to fix himself a sandwich, tinkers with the phonograph, succumbs weak-mindedly to the pages of a magazine, drifts off into an erotic reverie. But a walk, besides preventing such intrusions, unlocks the subconscious in such a way as to allow the writer to feel his mind spilling over with ideas. He is able to carry on the essential dialogue with himself in an atmosphere as intimate as a confessional, though his body hurries onward at three miles an hour. Without a daily walk and the transactions it stimulates in my head, I would face that first page of cold blank paper with pitiful anxiety.

I am lucky to have, in the colder part of the year, a house in the New England countryside, and in the summer a place by the sea. Thus on my walks I am exposed to manifestations of Nature in several of its most seductive moods; the aspects of pleasure and survival I mentioned are connected with being able to walk through serene, lovely, unpolluted landscapes while at the same time feeling throughout my body a diurnal blessing. As any knowledgeable doctor will testify, walking three to six miles or more at a steady pace—fast, energetic, taxing one's self but not to the point of exhaustion—is a motor activity of the most beneficial sort; privately, it is my view that any more arduous form of perambulation (for the middle-aged nonathlete, at least) must be a danger.

A case in point—perhaps more meaningful because this narrative is about warfare, and specifically the marines—would be my recollection of Major General Brenton Forbes, United States Marine Corps, whose poignantly familiar countenance peered out at me from the top of the obituary page of the *New York Times* one summer morning in the mid-1970s. The face of General Forbes, then in his early fifties and recently photographed (one could see the two stars on his epaulet), was the same face, only slightly larded over by the flesh of maturity, of Private "Brent" Forbes, who had shared with me a double-decker bunk at the Parris Island boot camp in 1944. The magisterially handsome man with the heavy eyebrows and humorous eyes and dimpled chin was the grown-up boy who had been the star recruit and superjock in our college-bred platoon, crack rifle shot and natural leader, inevitably destined to make the Marine Corps his career. It is striking how, if one is at all attentive, one rarely loses sight of the trajectory of the brilliant friends of one's youth, and later I had seen Forbes's name celebrated more than once: during the Korean War, in which as a captain he had won the Medal of Honor, and as a regimental commander in Vietnam, where by way of television one evening I saw, to my exquisite surprise, good old Dicnt standing beneath the whirling blades of a helicopter, pointing out something on a map to Henry Kissinger. The obituary stunned me—so young, so soon! Now the gorgeous ascent had been arrested close to its zenith, and the commanding general of the First Marine Division, Camp Pendleton, California, had dropped dead, found sprawled on the back lawn of his house in his *jogging clothes!*

I don't mean to mock the dead—a residual part of me admires such a man—but I can't help thinking that a program of walking, not jogging, would have allowed him to be alive today. Besides, there is something about jogging that is too trendy, verging on the effete; certainly it is *un-marine*. It is inconceivable that an old-time marine general—Smedley Butler, for instance, that salty old warrior of the early decades of the century—would have ever donned the uniform of a jogger. Walking, yes. Butler was as tough an egg as was ever hatched and—so the chronicles have it—an inveterate walker. Thus one does not visualize him jogging or, God forbid, running; one fancies him, rather, striding purposefully through some Coolidge-era dawn at Quantico or San Diego, thinking important thoughts about the destiny of the Corps, or of Caribbean skirmishes in bygone days, and the tidy machine-gun emplacements, and the bodies of Haitians and Nicaraguans mingled with those of his own beloved marines. Jogging would have appeared to Butler an absurdity, not only because the added exertion is unseemly and unnecessary (and, as we have just seen, sometimes lethal) but because it precludes thinking. Many of history's original and most versatile intellects have been impassioned walkers who, had speedier locomotion appeared to be a desirable adjunct to the idea of *mens sana in corpore sano,* would surely have adopted it, and so it is grotesque to think of Immanuel Kant, Walt Whitman, Einstein, Lincoln, Amiel, Thoreau, Vladimir Nabokov, Emerson, Tolstoy, Matthew Arnold, Wordsworth, Oliver Wendell Holmes, George Gissing, John Burroughs, Samuel Johnson, or Thomas Mann ajog. "Intellectual activity," wrote Nathaniel Hawthorne, "is incompatible with any *large amount* of bodily exercise." The italics are mine, but they could as well have been supplied by Hawthorne, who was a notorious devotee of walking.

But enough of that. Because it may be already apparent, I have not mentioned an aspect of walking that for me, at least, is absolutely essential: one must be alone. There are communal walks that are fun, but I am not referring to these, only to the ones where some sort of creativity can take place. Here a dog may be a welcome exception to the rule of solitude; one's dog—whose physiology prevents it from being a chatterbox—can be a wonderful companion, making no conversational demands while providing an animated connection with one's surroundings. On a walk the writer doesn't want to get so totally absorbed in his thoughts that he loses sight of the countryside; despite the rewarding trancelike periods I have mentioned, one must also enjoy the scenery—otherwise an indoor treadmill would suffice. This is where Aquinnah becomes important to me—important as I am to her, I might add, since her enthusiasm for walking is persistent and obvious, verging on the frantic as she waits for the stroll. The offspring of a black Labrador sire and an incredibly sweet-tempered golden retriever, she acquired her mother's tawny hue plus a large measure of her gentle saintliness, while the paternal genes gave her pluck and boisterousness. At the risk of an absurd anthropomorphism, I must say that the result is a bit like an amalgam of Mother Teresa and Muhammad Ali: moral grandeur and fierce tomfoolery in one beast, with just a touch of the lunacy of each model.

Aquinnah—the name is Wampanoag Indian from Martha's Vineyard—has been surgically deprived of her capacity for motherhood, and the transformation has made her neither less feminine nor rudely masculine but somehow pleasantly androgynous, mixing all the maddening and beguiling singularities of both sexes: timorousness and reckless courage; an almost feline fastidiousness combined with the gross corruption of a creature whose greatest joy is to dive, sleazily grinning, from a hayloft into a towering pile of cow manure; a docile homebody one day and a swaggering wanderer the next—and so on. I delight in the remarkable variety of Aquinnah's many natures—never more so than on our hundreds of walks together, whether she be trotting ladylike by my side or streaking out across a field for some prey that her nose detects far more quickly and surely than my vision. At that instant, with her caramel hair abristle and her white muzzle glued to the spoor, she appears to my somewhat nearsighted eyes as fierce and as fleet as a lioness of the Serengeti, although I must confess that not once, not a single time, has she tracked down so much as a chipmunk.

—Previously unpublished, CA. 1985

"IN VINEYARD HAVEN"

ONCE AT A SUMMER COCKTAIL PARTY IN MENEMSHA
I was asked by a lady: "Where on the island do you live?"

"In Vineyard Haven," I replied.

She suddenly gave me a look that made me feel as if I
harbored a communicable disease. "My God," she said, "I
didn't think anyone *lived* there."

Well, people do live there, and the moment of the year
that I look forward to with unsurpassed anticipation is
when I roll the car off the ferry, negotiate the fuss and confusion of the dock area, wheel my way past the homely
façade of the A&P, twist around down Main Street with its
(let's face it) unprepossessing ranks of mercantile empori-
ums, and drive northward to the beloved house on the
water. On an island celebrated for its scenic glories, Vineyard Haven will never win a contest for beauty or charm;
perhaps that's partly why I love it. The ugly duckling
gains its place in one's heart by way of an appeal that is not

immediately demonstrable. The business district is a little tacky, but why should it be otherwise? It is neither more nor less inspiring than other similar enclaves all across the land. People often think they yearn for quaintness, for stylishness, for architectural harmony; none of these would be appropriate to Vineyard Haven, which thrives on a kind of forthright frowziness. A few years ago, an overly eager land developer—now mercifully departed from the island— was heard proclaiming his desire to transform downtown Vineyard Haven into a "historical" site, similar to the metamorphosis effected by Mr. Beinecke on Nantucket. It is good that this plan came to naught. How silly and dishonest Cronig's Market and Leslie's Drug Store would look wearing the fake trappings of Colonial Williamsburg.

As for residential handsomeness, the good town of Tisbury cannot compete with Edgartown—that stuffy place; even so, had the lady from Menemsha walked along William Street or viewed more closely some of the dwellings lining the harbor, she would have discovered houses of splendid symmetry and grace. She would have also found some of the noblest trees lining the streets of any town its size on the eastern seaboard. It is this loose, amorphous "small townness" that so deeply appeals to me. A large part of the year, I live in a rural area of New England where one must drive for miles to buy a newspaper. The moors of Chilmark and the lush fens of Middle Road then, despite their immense love-liness, do not lure me the way Vineyard Haven does. I like the small-town sidewalks and the kids on bikes and the tres-passing gangs of dogs and the morning walk to the post of-fice past the Café du Port, with its warm smell of pastry and coffee. I like the whole barefoot, chattering mêlée of Main Street—even, God help me, the gawping tourists with their Instamatics and their avoirdupois. I like the preposterous gingerbread bank and the local lady shoppers with the Down East accents, discussing bahgins.

Mostly I love the soft collision here of harbor and shore, the subtly haunting briny quality that all small towns have when they are situated on the sea. It is often manifested simply in the *sounds* of the place—sounds unknown to forlorn inland municipalities, even West Tisbury. To the stranger, these sounds might appear distracting, but as a fussy, easily distracted person who has written three large books within earshot of these sounds, I can affirm that they do not annoy at all. Indeed, they lull the mind and soul, these vagrant noises: the blast of the ferry horn—distant, melancholy—and the gentle thrumming of the ferry itself outward bound past the breakwater; the sizzling sound of sailboat hulls as they shear the waves; the luffing of sails, and the muffled boom of the yacht club's gun; the eerie wail of the breakwater siren in dense fog; the squabble and cry of gulls. And at night to fall gently asleep to the far-off moaning of the West Chop foghorn. And deep silence save for the faint *chink-chink*ing of halyards against a single mast somewhere in the harbor's darkness.

Vineyard Haven. Sleep. Bliss.

—*The New York Times Magazine,* 15 JUNE 1980

WILLIAM STYRON (1925–2006), a native of the Virginia Tidewater, was a graduate of Duke University and a veteran of the U.S. Marine Corps. His books include *Lie Down in Darkness, The Long March, Set This House on Fire, The Confessions of Nat Turner, Sophie's Choice, This Quiet Dust, Darkness Visible,* and *A Tidewater Morning.* He was awarded the Pulitzer Prize for Fiction, the Howells Medal, the American Book Award, the Légion d'Honneur, and the Witness to Justice Award from the Auschwitz Jewish Center Foundation. With his wife, the poet and activist Rose Styron, he lived for most of his adult life in Roxbury, Connecticut, and in Vineyard Haven, Massachusetts, where he is buried.